MW01265288

HOPE
from
Violence—
A True Story

Religious Poetry

Cindy,

It was lovely the spirit
in you lit up the room
et my life.

DARLENE JAMISON

Darlene Jamison

Copyright © 2020 Darlene Jamison
All rights reserved
First Edition

PAGE PUBLISHING, INC.
Conneaut Lake, PA

First originally published by Page Publishing 2020

ISBN 978-1-6624-1847-1 (pbk)
ISBN 978-1-6624-1849-5 (digital)

Printed in the United States of America

SPECIAL THANKS

This book is dedicated to the first responders and volunteers who put their lives on the line for people every day. We thank them for their selfishness and care that they so diligently give to people. It hurts my heart when first responders lose their lives trying to help others. They do what a lot of us can't or won't do. The law enforcement, fire department, paramedics/EMTs, and also the volunteer first responders must all be added in our prayers every day. Where would we be without them? None of us are perfect. We can't let bad experiences interfere with all first responders in our prayers and thoughts. Just like us civilians, we are grateful we have first responders in our time of need. They are right there for us no matter what they have to face, and this is courage. There are good and bad in all professions of life. Don't judge all the first responders for the actions of a handful. We must learn to help and not be a hinder to professionals who are there to help us. Look out for them and be thankful for those who put their lives on the line every single day. Sometimes a heartfelt card will brighten their spirits and feel appreciated.

Also, my friend Michael Andrews encouraged me to write my first book. Mike is an intelligent and conscientious man. We used to work together at a few long-term care facilities. I was standing at the nurse station one day, discussing how hard it was to get my first poetry book published. Michael was passing by that day and said, "Darlene, you're a nurse and an artist. Just publish it yourself."

With that being said, I listened. He had a lot to do with me publishing my first self-published book of poetry. Michael Andrews is a registered nurse. He is excellent in this field. I can personally say he would be excellent in any field he chooses. When I first became a nurse, he was my director of nursing at one time. I learned a lot from him, and he taught me a lot. In fact, I can say he made me the nurse that I had become before retiring. A few other good nurses I learned a lot from too. I was professional and accurate, and I cared about my patients and others. Professionalism was engraved in Mike's heart and eyes, and he probably doesn't know it, but that also engraved me to be a better person and a better me in my field and also in life. We have been friends for over twenty years. Wow, time goes fast, so be the best you can be while you are young and teach others and even give them constructive criticism. This will make a better you if you listen when it is being taught to you.

INTRODUCTION

I wrote this book to inspire and teach people about the violence that so many of us across America and around the world have experienced violence in their lives and hope that you don't have to experience any sort of violence. Most importantly it is my hope and dream for parents from all walks of life and all races to read to evaluate everything in our lives to make things a better place to live without the violence.

Violence has existed for centuries the first violent act was at the beginning of time when Adam and Eve had two sons. One of the brothers was jealous of the other brother and killed him. This was the evil that was within him to kill his own brother. This is all in the Bible about how the brother Cain killed his brother Abel. (Genesis 4:8).

Jealousy and hate go together they are both hand in hand you can't have one without the other. Cause jealousy leads to hate and ignorance is sometimes a seed in a person. Ignorance is rolled up in a variety of unpleasantly things but this can all be changed in one if they choose to do so. There are two words that are vital to ourselves which is right or wrong. Sure we're all not perfect (*only God the Father, God the Son and God the Holy Spirit are perfect*) but just because each and every one of us are not perfect we do know the difference between right and wrong. Which is that inner spirit in all of us. My hope is that this book will help and understand life as it unfolds throughout our lives. Hope, dreams and goals are something we must strive for so that we can find favor from Jesus, who will help and guard us against evil that is in this world.

Reading is golden and more golden especially when we are taught about The Bible. The Bible is full of understanding, knowledge, hope, wisdom and most importantly is respecting His words. Sure we all make mistakes and don't always do what Jesus ask us to do…why…because we are not perfect or always right. So this is why God had The Bible written and it is the only Book that has been in the world for centuries and will always exist. If you think about this for a moment by this you will know that He created His Words for us to never go away no matter who has tried in centuries all the way to the current days to forbid His Book. (The Holy Bible).

I will not preach to you but I will tell you my inner spirit prompted me to write this book. I will write from A to Z how to have hope for a better future for our lives and our family and friends lives. So I thank you for reading this book. It starts at home and responsibility falls on each and every one of us as individuals in all races that's it's never too late to grow up even if we are adults. Also to face the truth and responsibility that all of us must carry. Yes, I said adults…'cause some adults have not grown up as well, so how do one expect their children to grow up to be educated hard working adults. Like I said it starts in the home whether it is a two parent household or a one parent household either one is doable. One must be consistent and determined to mold our children into educated and respectable people.

THE BEGINNING

I brought two children in the world. One is a girl and the other is a boy. But they are adults now with families of their own. In reality, in my life now, I have four boys and three daughters that whom I did not bring in the world, but I love them just as if I had. So I can say I have nine adult children whom love me as much as I love them. It is not the job of the teachers at school or the police officers to raise our children. It is the teacher's job to educate our children at school but our job to educate them at home. It is not the police officer's job to tell your children they should be at home instead of on the streets where they could get into trouble with the law or get harmed or worse, but it is our parents' job to keep a watchful eye over our children and know where they are at all times. When my children were young in grade school, sometimes I would not let myself be seen by them. I would do this to watch over them for their safety to make sure no one would bother my children or anyone else's children.

As parents, we have to do whatever it takes to keep our children safe from harm. After my children became adults, I told them how I used to sneak and watch them at the bus stop to make sure they got on safely. They laughed and one of them said, "I have a feeling you were somewhere around, Mom," and we would laugh. Know your children's destination and arrival time at home, and know who they are with at all time. One must keep a tight rein of discipline and love for their children at all times, and you must be diligent in doing so. Thank you for purchasing this book, *Hope from Violence*.

I'm going to start this true story about a young teenager in this book. That teenager was me. You will read about how this real-life experience as a young, fourteen-year-old teenager at that time who went through trials and tribulations. This true story of mine will help, teach, and encourage you how I was able to survive in life from a violent man in a treacherous neighborhood. My brother, Oliver Lee Sims Sr., told me I should put this true event in this book because it would help other teenagers from becoming victims.

When I was fourteen years old, walking from the hospital with my friend (I will call her Mary and she was also fourteen years old) because Mary had an asthma attack, a man in his late twenties came out of a meat market store with a butcher apron on. He asked Mary for her phone number, and she told him no because he was too old for her. After all, we were only teenagers. So the man grabbed Mary around her neck and was choking her as she was showing him her asthma inhaler. He knocked the inhaler out of her hand onto the ground. I tried to pull his arm off her neck, but he was too strong. She told the man she can't breathe. He pushed me down in the mud and continued to choke her. I had to save her. I was so angry that he messed up all the curls in my hair. That took me an hour to curl because I had long hair. I always kept my hair curled every day to always look my best. I was angry both ways because he was choking her to death and had messed up my hair with mud. But I knew I had to get the man off Mary before he killed her.

I saw a brick lying in the mud, and I started beating him on the head to get him off her. It destabilized him from standing up on both legs. Once I got him down to the ground with the brick, I continued to beat his entire head. I knew if the grown man got up, he would hurt us because he was a big adult male. So I kept beating him because I was afraid he'd get up. He was going to kill me 'cause I was just scared. Mary had run off and left me and yelled down the street to me, "You're killing him!" I heard her voice, but it was like time had stood still, and her voice sounded distant. Then she had to pull me off him so the man wouldn't die. That's when I came back to reality and saw all the blood on my hands and clothes. I got up because he was out and unconscious.

We left the man on the muddy park, and there were at least fifty people standing around, watching. We were teenagers. We didn't know what to do, so I went to her house and washed my hair and my body, and she gave me something to wear. Later, we walked to the store to get potato chips and Pepsi. Mary said, "Look at all of these police cars outside of the store we were in." And she said, "They are going to arrest somebody."

Little did I know it was going to be me. The police brought a man in stiches, staples, had open wounds, black eyes, and a bandage wrapped around his head. Also many of his teeth were broken or missing. Almost all of his teeth were missing. I didn't know who he was. Well, it was the man that was choking Mary, the man that I had beaten with a brick. I knew this 'cause he told the police officer, pointing at me, that I was the one who did this to him. His exact words were "I'll never forget her eyes."

People tell me to this day that my eyes are what's striking to them for some reason. To this day, I still hear the same thing about my eyes, that stand out. But they're the same eyes that I've always had, and I don't see anything remarkable about them.

Well, there was hope and faith that day. God gave me this strength to beat the man off Mary. So learn from me. If you are ever grabbed or if someone is trying to hurt or kill you, use any means necessary to save your life. If you are ever grabbed, scan your surroundings to see what you can use to stop someone from hurting or killing you, then use that object to defend yourself. The police arrested me and Mary because the man had lied to the police, saying that I had attacked him for no apparent reason and that he had never choked anyone. After about an hour of sitting in jail with handcuffs on, the police looked at us two skinny teenagers and got the man to tell the truth what really happened. The police told us before releasing us that they had to call our parents to pick us up. I knew my mother was going to be angry after the police said "Your mom wants to talk to you." I explained that it was self-defense, but she was angry anyway. She said, "I told you to stop hanging around that ugly girl," and "She doesn't like you anyway."

Well, mom knows best because the friend, Mary, started a lot of chaos with other people our age to try to cause negative division. My mom was right! I don't like violence, but you have to defend yourselves, so ask God to give you the power and the strength to make it out alive, and He will give it to you. That could have been us dead or injured. But I have a feeling to this day that the man will never bother teenage girls anymore after his almost-death ordeal. Never give up hope that you can make it out alive from any type of violence. I'm alive today due to me never giving up hope from violence even though Mary ran off and left me while I was fighting this grown man. Well, this is something she will have to live with. Everyone, let me tell you that if you help someone from violence and that person is supposed to be a friend and doesn't help you fight off a grown man, this means they are not your friend. Cut them off for life and leave them alone because this will only hurt yourself in the long run from being friends with a coward who was fighting her fight against a strong adult male.

I told my godbrother about this story, and he encouraged me to put it in this book. My godbrother's name is Oliver L. Sims. He is closer than a blood brother, and he is a good and honest man whose family I am blessed to be a part of. Oliver told me that this book would help other young teenage girls get away from an attacker. This book is to learn, listen, and know about the violence that exists in our era in order to protect ourselves and to protect our loved ones. Oliver has always been an inspiration and help in my life. This is why he is my big brother. He is a very kind and intelligent man with wisdom that he so freely shares with others if they choose to listen.

As time moved on, I met a very excellent and professional nurse who is an RN (registered nurse). This nurse held many medical field-related titles behind her name, besides being an RN. I asked her why she didn't sign all her documentation with her titles. Her response made me sad. She said, "If I sign my other titles, some people would get jealous and give me a hard time at work, and she had too many bad experiences as a nurse to go through that again." I informed her that God blessed her to earn these titles and that she should not hide anything that God has blessed her with. The truth is that Jesus does not want the blessings He gives to be hidden. God wants others to know that He is the giver of blessings so that they can believe in Him and praise Him. Jesus rewards us and gives us a gift that no one else can give. That is the gift of an everlasting life with Him.

Some may wonder why I sometimes write God or Jesus throughout this book. God, Jesus, and the Holy Spirit are three in one. He is the Alpha and the Omega. He is the beginning and the end.

This book does not reflect on one individual; it reflects on many aspects of all people's lives. I hope this inspirational poems will enable you to understand and deal with many aspects of life. My inspiration comes from Jesus, who enabled me to write this book. I can't take credit for anything in life because all praise, glory, and credit go to the giver of life, Jesus. He will touch your life and have you do certain works for people.

There will be poems in this book that are true, and these poems came from my life, others' lives, and things I have learned from life itself. They are meant to help, encourage, strengthen, and give you faith in Jesus Christ.

Some of my family, friends, and people in general have experienced violence in their lives just as I had. But we must always have hope from violence. Without hope, where would the world of people be?

A TRUE STORY

Let's start with the home and in our home. Home is a place to live for yourself or your family. We have to be diligent in teaching our children right from wrong in their early years and on. If you believe in God, teach your children about Him and have weekly readings from the Bible to your family in the living room, dining room, or whatever room you choose that is comfortable for your children so that they will hear, listen, and take in what is being taught to them.

Also talk to them about how to behave indoors and outdoors. Teach them to respect the law, teachers, others, and their home. Most importantly, respect the parents so that they will know that if they do the wrong thing, there will be consequences to be dealt with, and you should explain the consequences to them. Unfortunately, this is not being done in some of the homes.

It is never too late to change and ask God for forgiveness for our sins. He says so in the holy Bible, and He is a God of His words. Some people will say you can't believe everything in the Bible 'cause they are fixated that man has changed it. If you read the last part of Revelations, He said that if anyone try to change or add to His book, they will suffer all the plagues that is in the entire Bible. So only you can decide which way you will go.

We are living in violent times in our society, and we must do our part as parents to prevent our children from becoming violent or being a victim of violence. Some children are raising themselves on the streets or at hangout places.

Parents, adults, and leaders of communities with these drug-infested and shooting-infested neighborhoods. Talk with the adults even if you have to hold public meetings. When you talk to the adults about their children or others, this will trickle down, and prayerfully make the heads of a household responsible for the part they should be doing. Don't be afraid and turn your head unless you want Jesus to turn His head on you on Judgment Day.

We are all born, and eventually death is evident 'cause we are born to do good and help others, and there will be a day for all of us to expire. We are judged on what we do by God, so let it be that we do be good. It is never too late to change. If you ask for forgiveness and are truly sorry, He will forgive you, and it will be remembered no more according to the Bible. God is the only one whom we can have trust in.

Parents, when your children kill, rob, harm, or commit any violent act against another person(s), don't say "My child will never do that." The fact is no one knows what their child is capable of, and that is in any race. Have you searched his room, accessed the internet, and known of their whereabouts? If you have said this to yourself or others, ask yourself if you have done some of the parenting things we should be doing to check and see what they are doing.

Invest our children into resisting racism and violence, and ensure peace in their surroundings. If you directly or indirectly talk of hate of any race, our children will hear this and carry it with them. There is good and bad in every profession—not one but all professions. I've even experienced good and bad in my medical profession. We need to support our police officers 'cause not all are corrupt and full of hate.

I had a bad experience with a police officer when I was fourteen years old. I was standing outside, talking with two friends, when a police officer pulled up, made us get in his car, and told us he was taking us to a drug store to be identified as robbers. The officer wouldn't let us tell our parents what was happening to us innocent teens. He just demanded we get in his car, and we didn't know if he was taking us to do harm to us or what.

We arrived at a drug store, and he took the three of us in and asked the lady behind the counter, "Was this the three that robbed you?" The lady said no, and the officer asked us if we wanted him to drop us back off where he picked us up. I was a very outspoken person, so I said, "No." We rather walk back home than to be the car with him. I was angry and embarrassed and more upset that he didn't tell our parents where we were. In spite of that, this did not make me angry at all law officials. Sometimes, to fix a problem, you have to make things better like perhaps by growing up and becoming a law official or growing up to get an education and a respectful employment. If one fixates themselves on negativity and no positivity, then he/she loses in life. Their whole life will become a waste.

Be an asset, not a waste. There is hope if you have the right tools to teach you and work with you. We must support all first responders and our firefighters who put their lives on the line to extinguish fires and save lives inside burning buildings. The fire department also deliver free smoke detectors. When the batteries are out, what are we going to do? Call the fire department for batteries? Use your common sense, and go buy batteries and teach your children not to play with matches or anything that can cause fires. These teachings will save many lives in our families and the fire department. When we are in need of saving our health and help, we call the EMTs/paramedics, and they come and perform lifesaving techniques. What about our volunteer first responders? They work with their heart to help and save lives. Some say there are no jobs, but there are plenty of jobs. They may not be the jobs you want, but you have to start somewhere and build your career from there.

The possibilities are high when you work toward your education. If you have a dream, make it real. If you have hope, make it more hopeful. If you have a goal or goals, strive and make that goal a reality. Stay away from people who will tell you that you won't make it. Anyone who tells a person that is a loser and doesn't want to see you win in life. Any accomplishment, award, and hard work is a winner. If you are the head of a household and the neighborhood and the environment is ridden with violence, this means it is the work of much evil. Move away from it to enhance your family life and well-being. You may have to work and attend college. Just remember that you're never too old to make changes in your life and your family life. Start making positive moves and changes today—not tomorrow but today! Believe and have faith in the Lord, in Jesus, and He will make miracles in your life and your family's lives as well. Jesus told us to ask and we shall receive. Now, this does not mean it will happen this very minute. It will come on His time when He knows the right way and time for His children. We're human, so let Him and allow Him to make positive, good spiritual changes in our lives on earth. Of course we're going to make mistakes. We all do. But we should learn from our mistakes and not make them twice and teach others so they, too, will learn. Let those with two ears listen and let those with the Holy Spirit feel it and act upon it.

Please allow me to help those who want help with the best credit repair company there is across the states. The name of the company is Synergy Credit Services. They are located at 2821 S. Parker Road (suite 265) in Denver, Colorado, 80014. Their email address is synergycreditpros.com. No matter what state you live in, they will help you to repair and build your credit. I can speak professionally highly of them from my own personal experience. Some people will not share information to help others, but I am here to help anyone who want to help themselves. I worked with Mr. Nate Eubank at Synergy Credit Repair for only four months, and if you follow his directions, you, too, can repair or build your credit score. I never thought this would happen, but it did. This is why I am recommending you to contact this company. They work hard and are diligent in helping the people. Professionalism at all times are given to us. Their fees are so reasonable. You can do this even on a fixed income, and you won't be disappointed. You'll be able to move yourself or your family to where you want to be. I was assigned to Nathaniel Eubank to help me repair my credit. All the Synergy Credit Repair representatives and the owner, with love in their hearts and soul to help people. I can say this from personal experience with Nate (Nathaniel Eubank). I had grown to love this young man and his company, and the feelings were mutual, not fake or misleading like other credit repair companies. Their work is sincere, and they consider their customers with love. Make that call today, and spread this information to help others because it is a must. You receive in life what you have given out in life, and it is never too late to do the right thing to help others.

I had suffered an on-the-job lifetime injury. It was hard to find an attorney who would help me since I was no longer able to work as a nurse or any kind of job. I was stuck with a lifetime of chronic pain and will still do for the rest of my life. I met the most professional, diligent, and caring attorney at his law firm.

ATTORNEY DANIEL J. GAUTHIER, LLC
mylegalworld@sbcglobal.net

When I met Daniel J. Gauthier, he had experience and intelligence in his eyes, and I knew I was in good hands with his law firm after suffering through trials and nonstop tribulations for years. Mr. Gauthier and the law firm secretary, Lindzie Littlefield, were my rock for years until I was compensated for my lifetime injury. It took years and all the legal work and appeals for this to happen. But Mr. Gauthier never gave up. This is one of the God's gifts that was given to him since birth. As years passed, while waiting to overcome my almost poverty level, Mr. Gauthier and Lindzie and I became friends. My heart began to heal through the years of suffering because whenever I needed someone to talk to, the both of them never turned their ear away from me. They knew just about everything of my personal and professional life. To this day, they are friends whom I can trust.

Even so, Gauthier and Littlefield stood by my side through many of the things that happened in my life. That's when I knew they would be friends for life in my heart. If someone ever need an attorney for an injury and other things, call the best law firm in Missouri. He also helps people in other states as well. This is the man to call: Daniel J. Gauthier, attorney at law. He also travels out of state to defend and help all his clients. I can speak from personal experience; I would not have made it without his law firm. Need a professional and ethical attorney? Contact them, and you, too, will be in good hands. Mr. Gauthier and his law firm worked for me for six years without receiving a dime from me until his law firm brought everything to a closure for me with the compensation that I so desperately needed. The point is, Gauthier is not a quitter. He is a fighter for what is right. I would recommend Gauthier law firm to anyone and everyone.

Adults must protect their children at all times. Never let them walk to the store alone or the bus stop alone. In reality, never let your children go off anywhere alone because the times we are living in are dangerous times for children and adults. In case of emergency, if you're ever caught in a violent situation, you must use all necessary means to your disposal to get away, and yell where people can hear you. Take self-defense classes. Talk to your local police departments to have a discussion with a law official on self-protection in order to live and get away from any violent situation. It's always good to be prepared just in case violence ever comes your way. You can always start neighborhood watch programs. The law officials are here to help the public, but we have to communicate to let them know our concerns. Nothing can be fixed unless it is communicated to be repaired. If you have to move your family out of crime-ridden neighborhoods and if credit is a problem, you already have the previous information of Synergy Credit Repair. That will help you as well. If you give up hope, then what will you have left?

Once we die, it's all over, so let your works on earth be good while we are alive. There is life after death. Believe me, I experienced life after death and I know. This is why I write true stories so others can learn from my mistakes or sins to help you to never give up 'cause whatever we do while we are alive, we are held accountable by it after death. So do the best we can to do the right thing and not the wrong thing, as the devil waits and nudges us to do the wrong things. Resist the devil and demand him to leave your presence in the name of Jesus. Have faith, and all will be okay. I'm not saying life will be peachy, but life will have its ups and downs. That's okay. It's just part of life. It's up to each individual which road he or she chooses to walk on. Remember, if it doesn't feel right…then it's not right. Go with your instincts and ask God to sharpen your instincts so you'll know when to take flight or when to fight. He will grant you this if you ask Him of it.

Some of my family members have experienced violence in their lives, and each were innocent victims. I myself have experienced violence in my life as well. One family member was taking his daily walk for exercise and one day, while he was out walking, a group of four men (cowards) tried to force him into a car while beating him and at the same time trying to push him into their car. God gave him the strength to push himself backward from the men, and they grew tired of trying to push him into the car and sped off. God gave him the strength he needed to resist the devils, which spared his life.

We must be aware of our surroundings at all times. Always hope for the best even when it seems as though there is no hope. This will make you stronger in many aspects of our lives. Have inspiration, and pass inspiration to others in and out of your circle. Sometimes when we make mistakes in life, this can be our best teacher so we won't do it again. Be careful in giving your trust to others. This does not mean to become distrustful to everyone 'cause you have to go with your instincts. If it doesn't feel right, then it's probably not right.

Two of my family members were shot, and thanks to God, they survived from the intentional murderous acts of a couple of cowardly evil people. Talking turned into a shooting. The shooters were caught and convicted and served time. The chances are when they are released, they'll probably shoot more innocent victims. The legal system will change to harder and harsher time for these cowards who act like animals. This is why we must support our police officers. People who say they hate the police are lost souls, and when they need help, who do they call? They call the police and expect the police to help when you say you hate them. It takes a strong-minded and courageous person to be a police officer. They put their lives on the line every day for us. Not all police are bad. There are more good cops than bad cops. You will find this in every profession where there is good and bad. I support and pray for our officers. This is called love and hope.

Yes, prejudice does exist, and it has existed for centuries. We all can teach our children, families, friends, and others not to judge a book by its cover until we read the contents. If you see or feel evil around, get away from the surroundings and pray to Jesus to remove it. Jesus said to ask and we shall receive, and from personal experience, this is true. A few women became jealous because they saw a picture of me with a medical doctor who had written a book. This particular doctor asked me (he knew I was an artist) to draw the illustration for the cover of his book. Then these evil, beastly women attacked me outside with a knife, yelling "You're not the only one who has talent!" while stabbing me several times.

This is not the first time. This has been said to me through the years. I was fighting back so hard that I hadn't realized I had been stabbed several times 'cause I was trying to protect my life and was hoping I could make it out of that alive. I was in my early forties and so were the attackers. People were watching, but not one person among the onlookers called the police.

Some people just like violence and see it as entertainment. These are sick-minded individuals. They have no hope, no job, no remorse, and no goodness within them. They cling to evil and hate as if it were their best friend. God gave me the strength to walk to a house next door and ask them to call an ambulance and the police. The neighbor looked in horror. I hadn't realized that I had lost a copious amount of blood and couldn't move my right arm; it was severed all the way to the bone. These cowards had planned to kill me because their jealousy had turned to hate and they wanted blood. If I had followed my first instincts, I would not have walked that way pass the house. I would have crossed the street and walked to a friend's house. Always go with your gut instincts 'cause it will save your life and perhaps save someone else's life. Thanks to God, the ambulance came and rushed me to the emergency room, and they were able to save my life from all the stab wounds. The gutless culprits were arrested at the scene. All the police officers at the scene were helpful except for one, and a decade later, he was on the news for wrongdoing and resigned. So you see, you don't have to retaliate anyone 'cause when you are wrong and do wrong, it will be addressed sooner or later by God. You don't have to lift a finger. Justice will be served for all wrongdoers and will be done on God's watch.

These thugs of all races use their hands and fingers to make gang signs and communicate with each other. Just think about it. They could attend college and become an asset to the community and the world if they would learn how to do sign languages for the mute and the deaf and teach it to them. This is a waste of talent. Everyone is blessed with talents and gifts, and some never use it nor want it.

Don't say it's hard being black to succeed anything in life. Many black people have ignored this type of mentality and have made great lives for themselves and their families. Let's take a look at history in the 1800s. Madam C.J. Walker was the first millionaire in America. Despite being a black woman, she overcame the unthinkable hurdles and she kept going and helped thousands of other people along the way all the way 'til she died in 1911. Look up the history of Madame C.J. Walker. This will inspire you. She did not abandon her gifts and talents which was given to her by God. She used them to the fullest as we all should. To this day, you can still order her hair products at Madam C. J. Walker. She also invented the pressing comb for black women. She was brilliant.

Read about her history, and if this does not inspire you, then you are just wasting your own gifted talents. Read, people, so you can learn, teach, and help others. This is what Jesus wants us to do, and there is no age limit on learning. Break away from people who are leading you down a path of destruction, violence, and death, even if it means having to move out of the environment and putting yourself in school. If you don't have a high school diploma, that is no problem. There are schools that will teach you for free to obtain your (GED) high school diploma. So, you see, there are no excuses. The only excuse you have is that you excuse yourself from being a prominent citizen. We cannot change what's happened in the past that's why there is a word named *forward*. In order to make changes, you have to move forward. We may not forget, but we can forgive to move on in our lives.

When Jesus was crucified and murdered, He said out loud, "FORGIVE THEM, FATHER, FOR THEY KNOW NOT WHAT THEY DO." If He can forgive, then we should follow Him and forgive as well. We may not forget, but we can forgive. I know it's hard to forgive, but hate kills the soul and eventually yourself. There is life after death. Would you rather spend it in heaven or spend it in hell forever after we die? We are born to live and then to die. So make the best of things while we are living because we all—how we lived—will be held accountable on Judgment Day. Every dog has their day, and some dogs have years of karma. When people do evil things to others like rob, steal, and kill, these types of people act like untrained dogs and not humans. If you know anyone, even if it is a family member, who have murdered someone, please call Crime Stoppers. You can remain anonymous. We must get these animals off the streets. To ignore not report it to law officials or Crime Stoppers even while knowing the people who are committing violent acts will eat away at your heart and soul. So do the right thing and get these criminals off the streets. God has no use for cowards, so be of some use and be a hero for God and help innocent people.

There has always been a special place in my heart for innocent people, children, babies, law officers, military, fire department, and all first responders. We must always never forget the volunteers who are there for the people. These officials put their lives on the line every single day, and the majority respect that and them as well. Being a volunteer myself for many years, I also commend those who volunteer to help people in need. But I must admit that as per my experience as a volunteer nurse, some work from their heart whereas some work for show. This is nothing someone told me; this is something I've seen with my own eyes. In fact, during Hurricane Katrina, there was one white nurse who actually resigned because she didn't like a black woman (me) volunteering during that era of disaster. Not only was I told of this by our supervisor, but I have also seen the hate in that particular nurse who quit. In fact, the supervisor was thrilled by her own words that I was volunteering because she said I had a genuine heart and professionalism that could be clearly seen. To tell you the truth, even the black health-care profession that I worked with on my regular job as a nurse grew to despise me by saying a whole lot of things to spread rumors to those who would listen, saying "That bitch must think she's white… Only white people work for free." How ignorant and hateful!

Black—not all, but some—will hate you for evil jealousy in their hearts. What would they do if a disaster came in their life? Would they then say that or accept the volunteers who would help? Well, it happened in the majority of the city and county in the black community when there was an electrical outage for more than a week. Ninety percent of the shelter was set up for blacks and whites, and again, I volunteered. Ignoring how I was treated by my own race and giving 110% of myself during this crisis in St. Louis, I had to send many people out via ambulance for the ones who were dehydrated, and I cared for hundreds of people whom I treated all equally. They had no air, water, or food at their homes, and this is why they came to the shelter for help. To everyone's surprise, I was the only nurse there who worked tirelessly because I had to work at my job full-time as well. So I requested to work part-time so that I could devote my time before and after work to all the people in the cooling shelter. Also, I would teach universal precautions to all and did a lot of teaching of not spreading germs and on what and what not to do. You don't have to have money to volunteer. You can just use your skills to do so or even help cook, serve, and take people to the bathroom for those who have problems walking or just couldn't walk at all. There are so many things you can do in volunteering that I could probably write a book on.

We have some black people in the crime-ridden communities who are trying to help, teach, and make a difference. Instead of doing nothing, volunteer and help those who are trying to make a difference. Anyone can complain, but why complain when you can help yourself to help others? We've all made mistakes in our lives. But Jesus said that if you ask for forgiveness, it will be granted. Then forgive yourselves and move on from there. The only thing stopping you is yourself. Some people love to complain and put the blame on others for an excuse. Everyone in America had to start somewhere to make it to the top. So I say to those people that first, they have to start somewhere in any workplace and excel and make a career for themselves and continue to excel in any profession that they choose.

There is a lot of evil in the world. But one thing's for sure, good will always overcome evil. God is more powerful and all-powerful over everything. He will not continue to allow evil to dwell among His people and for evil people create more evil. If more families would teach their children about Him, I guarantee that there would be a better change for this world. Jesus is always present whether one chooses to believe it or not. He is watchful. We must always be vigilant and watchful for others, too, to help protect the innocent especially our children who cannot defend for themselves.

Some people are like snakes; they are poisonous and bite you without notice. You can see these things in their eyes which are the windows to what's in one's heart or intentions. Stay away from these kinds of people, even if you have to uproot yourself to a new environment and plant new roots that will blossom. Depression will set in if you allow yourself to stay in any evil or unsuitable situations.

Always hope for the best, but be prepared if anything or anyone goes south on you. What I'm trying to say is hope always strengthens the heart and soul. We all have done things in life that we are not proud of or wish we could have changed in the past. But we know we cannot change the past. This is why it's so important to teach our children at an early age about right and wrong so their future can glow and not be dim. This will also lower the suicide rate among our teens and young adults. I'm not a philosopher or have a master's degree in things, but God can master you in His way of knowledge and wisdom. All one has to do is allow Him to make these changes by opening up your heart to Him. This is something that no school can teach. Only the Teacher can give this to us so freely and willingly if we allow Him to. We are living in a spiritual warfare these days, and we have to allow Jesus to do things on His time and not our time.

Parents, get off your butts and go to your children's schools and make sure they are doing their work and not disrupting classrooms or terrorizing students, teachers, staff members, and others. Do this every week so your children will know there are consequences to be dealt with from their actions. Don't expect the teachers or police to raise your children; teaching and discipline start at home. Some parents act worse than their belligerent children when their children are disciplined by teachers or the police. Of course there are good and bad in all races and all professions. I am a witness to that. But does it help when some parents act as ignorant as some children do? Look in the mirror and what do you see? If you don't like what you see, then make a change.

Some children can grow up in the best of homes or the richest of homes and even to excellent parent(s). But they can just be a bad seed no matter what you do or don't do. Let's take Cain and Abel for instance. Cain murdered his brother Abel. Please read Genesis 4:8. I hear a lot from people about how God let things happen and why He doesn't stop horrific things from happening. I am not a minister, a preacher, or any kind of leader in the religious field. But has anyone stopped to think the evil one that does these things? We can't blame anything on God. We are all chosen a path, and not all of us take the path that we are so freely given by God. Yet we sometimes let Satan in and that is where our problems begin. The evil one will plant a seed and sow it if you allow it. If one plants a flower seed and nurture it, then it will blossom and become a beautiful flower. If one allows weeds to sow and don't plunk it out of the soil, it will continue to grow and be an ugly sight to look at. Take your soul for instance. If it is a good soul, it will flourish, and if it is a bad soul, it will kill the soul. Sometimes you can look into a person's eyes and will be able to see what is in his or her heart. Humans can't see the soul because it is spiritual, but what is in one's heart can be seen through their eyes. All around the world, the evil spirit is lurking and lurking harder into overtime at some neighborhoods. If you feel the spirit of evil lurking in your neighborhood, then you must get away from it, or it will possibly harm or kill you or even someone you love or care about. This requires hope, love, and faith in God to be able to feel or see these things. He will give it to you; all one has to do is ask. Jesus said to ask and it will be given. I firmly believe in this from my own personal experiences in life itself.

It all starts at home. If you teach and talk to your children about prejudice and derogatory teachings about other races, this will mold their minds into hating other races. People all around the world have derogatory thoughts about other races. How do they learn this? They learn it from home, family members, and friends. I have friends of all races and they feel free to talk to me about racism. I don't know why, but even people I barely know will talk to me about it. One white cashier told me that I'm a realist and that she feels comfortable talking to me. I try to keep an open mind and a willingness to teach others what I know so that they can spread the good word to their family, friends, and others. We have to make a difference no matter what race we are. Hope for the best, but be ready for the unexpected. Have the courage to speak out, and speak up when you see things being done that shouldn't be done or said. It's only teaching and we all can have something positive to elaborate on. But there is hope from violence. Be cautious and report any suspicious activities.

I was happy to hear that the St. Louis police departments are getting a raise. They deserve that and much more for what they do for the public and even strangers whom they protect. Like I said, there are good and bad in all professions in life, but there are more good cops than bad cops. There are good and bad in all professions. No one is perfect, but there are people who try to do the right thing more than the bad thing in life. This is called hope for our fellow human being.

Downtown St. Louis used to be an enjoyable place to go and take your family for a night out. I've been going downtown since I was a little girl, and when I had a family of my own, I used to take them there. The downtown tradition continued when my children became adults, but now a large percentage of people are afraid to go downtown. The violence and murders are so rapid and frequent that it is no longer safe. I can personally say that most of the violence is committed by evil people. There are a vast number of people—white, black, and other races—that have experienced violence downtown. People are arming themselves, and rightfully so, for protection. There is so much evil hovering in downtown that now these animals are shooting at the Metrolink train. An innocent man was shot in the back from running away from a man who had death in their soul.

The good news for hope is that the St. Louis police department are stepping in new directions to stop the violence. Their strategy is working and will continue to work for the public's safety. Sure, we hear a lot of bad things about cops, but there are good cops as well. There is good and bad in all professions in life. We, as the public, must and continue to support our law officials 'cause they are who we call when we need help and they put their lives on the line every day for us no matter what. Be respectful and helpful to them and remember that they are humans just like us and that they have feelings as we all do. We have good and bad days, and they have good and bad days. So keep this in mind when talking with an officer, and do as they direct us to do. They specialize in their field and are trained in what they do. In order to change any profession, one needs to obtain a job in that profession.

LIFE

The world has always been in a
Spiritual warfare.
That's why we must remain close to God.
Failure to do so is more than a scare.

Some people are prejudiced
And actually feel these things are right.
They feel if you're black, stay back
And if you're white, it's all right.

God created every man equal to His likeness.
This is in Genesis 1:27
Read it and open your heart
Because to believe is the only way to heaven.

I'm not just talking about black.
I'm not just talking about white.
I'm talking about people of all races.
Things can be dangerous if things are not done right.

Our law officials need help.
They don't need riots, chaos or to get shot.
Because at the end of the day
They, too, have a life not to die and rot.

Let the enemies die and rot
Not us who are trying to do right.
Get rid of the murderers
So we can all sleep at night.

Three weeks ago, my car stopped on me at the gas station. My towing service sent the wrong truck that only gave certain things like battery charges and such. They didn't send a tow truck as I had requested, as I was going to have it towed to a repair shop.

I told the driver that I had a bad feeling about being in this area and if he could call for a tow truck because the battery he gave me did not do the job. I knew it wasn't the battery. That's why I specifically asked for a tow truck when I first called. I elaborated to the driver from my towing club that I didn't feel safe here for some reason. Actually, it was the Holy Spirit that had sharpened my instincts. The driver told me he would wait with me 'til the tow truck arrived. I told him that it was up to him if he wanted to wait. I would be okay and it was okay for him to go ahead and leave. But he insisted on staying with me anyway.

While we were talking, a silver car pulled up and went around the back of the gas station. I asked him, "Where did that silver car go?" He said, "I think it went into the car wash." I told him, "No, it did not go into the car wash." I looked less than a minute and told the driver and there it was. The silver car had pulled in a spot close to the member driver which left me sandwiched in between both vehicles. I was sitting on the stoop, and the member driver was sitting in his truck on my left, and the silver car pulled up and parked to my right. Two black men got out and stood over me, and I immediately stood up and told the driver, "Okay, thank you very much, Sir, and have a good day," giving him the hint that it was time for him to go because these two guys were looking for trouble or worse.

So I went over to my car which was about a hundred feet from me. I opened up the car door and got my gun out. The member driver drove up next to my car door and he told me after I walked away that the two thugs started calling him names and using profanity words at him and that he also saw my gun. I allowed the driver to see it to let him know I had us protected. Then I put the gun next to my right thigh for easy access if the need arose.

In two seconds, one of the thugs walked up and was calling the man a cracker and insulting him, and the other thug was hiding on the other side of the worker's truck where he couldn't be seen. While one of the thugs was calling the man racial slurs, I couldn't see the other thug. I pointed my gun at the one I could see and told him to get away from that man, and I said, "Where's your buddy?" Then I said to member driver to "Go go go!" The driver screeched off as I had demanded him to because the thug I couldn't see was going to flank him. The two thugs ran off to their vehicle and screeched off. They were either going to rob us or kill us. But I turned the table on them.

When the tow truck driver came five minutes later, I explained to him what happened and told him to tell the other member driver to thank him for me. The unbelievable part was that my car started up when the tow driver turned the ignition key. I had hope and I had faith that the Lord was watching out for us, and He was. If you have hope, then you must have faith. But in my heart, I feel that change is coming for people who go out of their way to harm, hurt, steal from, and murder others. God will not let this continue to get worse for His innocent people, no matter what color you are, because He is a God who is merciful and will make the unjust have hell where their souls will go.

You're probably wondering how can she talk about God and the Bible. I love God the Father, God the Son and God the Holy Spirit, and I must always protect myself and the innocent while I'm on earth. Please read this poem below.

If you know anything about General George Patton, you will understand. If you don't know anything about General Patton, please read the history of him. Many of his men in World War II didn't understand how he was so intense with his religion with God and carried his special-made gun on his side. After reading this poem, you will get a little bit of his history.

A TRIBUTE TO PATTON

He stood over six feet tall.
His courage and wisdom were great.
He was a chosen leader
And was never late.
His heart was a sea of courage.
His mind was conditioned to winning wars.
His intelligence was known worldwide
As he battled under the glistening stars.
He led his men to combat
Fighting right by their side.
A general with three stars
And a Bible by his side worldwide.
He prayed on his knees
For victory and good weather throughout the war.
The men were confused
But prayed as they walked afar.
His name was General George S. Patton.
A man of honor, dignity and knowledge.
A great war hero
Who attended West Point Military College.
He foretold the coming of future events.
He knew the past as the future.
He was also a magnificent writer.
Who never came apart at the sutures.
All his victories were prosperous.
He knew this from the beginning.
Ignoring man's military orders.
He was adamant on winning.
He died of complications from an accident
After the war was over and won.
He fulfilled his destiny
After all was said and done.

Some things in life will probably get worse before they get better. But there is always hope and faith. Have faith in God. Have trust that He will end all this hatred, murder, and violence. Cling on to hope and faith, and this will save you. Sometimes it seems like your whole world is falling apart. I've been there before. But I hung on to faith and hope, and things did get better for me. Determination and not giving up hope will get us to where we need to be or need to be doing in life. God has given every person a gift or gifts. It's up to one if they choose to accept the gifts and use it for good or use it for evil. When they do, then one has thrown their gift(s) away. Some people are just born with an evil seed and can't sleep at night unless they have done evil. This is in the Bible, in the book of Proverbs.

So we must be relentless in teaching our children what is right and what is wrong all through their years of life. Teach them that they must be thorough in the good things they do in life to instill positivity and to avoid negativity. A two-parent household is always better than a one-parent household, but do the best that you can. We don't want our children to end up as a statistic. We want them to flourish and be prosperous in life with our guidance particularly on education and believing in ourselves that we and our children can do all things in life to become successful and respectable citizens in our community, family, others, and in the workplace. Some children need to hear how much and be shown how much we love them and want the best for them. This is nurturing the inner being to blossom.

When one falls upon hard times or have low income and you have to get assistance from the state or government, utilize this not as a lifelong term but as a stepping stool to step up that you no longer need assistance. Use that stepping stool and turn it into a ladder. A ladder is something to climb on. So climb up with education, life, employment, and many other aspects to build a life for you and your family. Some people take advantage and use it for a lifetime, and this is laziness along with other things such as low self-esteem and the equivalents that go along with laziness. I know many people with this type of mentality who feel like one is owed something in life to them without working for the things in life as others do. This type of irrational thinking trickles down to your offspring and others in their circle. If one fails to have hope and faith, then one fails to succeed in life. Without hope, it will put you in a depressive state of mind to be hopelessly lost. One should always want to gain to have that good feeling of strong diligence.

I can understand why people protest for various reasons. Decades ago, the protesters were not violent and protested for valid and good reasons. But in these times that we are living right now, there are always some unintelligible and disruptive beings who are defeating the purpose of the good protesters. For instance, just the other month in St. Louis, someone threw a water bottle at one of the news reporters for no reason. Throwing trash cans and breaking and destroying businesses. These business owners have done nothing to deserve their livelihood destroyed. They are working like a lot of us, trying to support and take care of their families and themselves. If some bad apples are going to destroy, why not destroy the thieves and murderers by turning them over to the law officials? You can always call Crime Stoppers, and you will remain anonymous, or go to another area in the city or county and make that call if you are afraid. The crime won't stop if you do nothing to turn these thugs in and get them behind bars where they belong.

This gang stuff has been going on for decades, and it is the silliest thing I have ever seen or heard of. You don't have to be in a gang. Go get a job and make something of yourself besides being an idiot. There is a place for these kinds of people—it's jail or hell. There are good and bad in all races, and no one is better than the other or above or below than the other, unless you put your own self there to become lower than a belly of a snake. If people continue to sit back down and raise hell every day, then you are nothing less than a heathen because you put yourself there. Even though racism does exist, that doesn't mean that you have to react on everything when you are confronted with it. I once lived in an all-white county and was the only black person living there. The prejudice and racism were shown by them, but once people got to know me and watch me, their attitudes changed, and they saw that people who are of a certain race are not all the same just because they have the same color of skin.

I broke the barrier because some of the people in the community saw the good that I was doing for all people of all races. That's when some of the confederate flags came down. If I addressed every little thing that was wrong or went wrong, how would the people see me then? They would have said, "See, I told you they're all alike." But this didn't happen. Instead some of the people were coming to me for help and for various types of help, and if I could help them, then I would. In fact, some of the people in that particular county asked me if I would help them with my skills that I had for various fundraisers for people in the community. The majority of the people have never lived around with other races so some of their rationale about certain races come from television. They became open to me and saw the difference I was making in people's lives and grew to watch out for me when I got off work so I could make it safely to my front door. They felt comfortable with me and had many questions about different races and other things. They would ask me about it, and I'd answer them honestly so they could learn and be more knowledgeable about certain things in life.

Enjoy your youth while you have it because one may think it will last forever but it won't. Learn all you can about the Holy Bible so as you grow older you will not have wasted your time trying to catch butterflies that you will never catch. Teach, learn, respect, and volunteer to help others. This is what we are supposed to do, and this is what Jesus expects for us to do. Failure to respect your parents or anyone else will lead to thirty times worse for people who are disrespectful to their parents. After all, they, too, will one day have children of their own and one reaps whatever they sow. So if you are a person like this, hold on tight. You are in for the slippery ride of your life of disrespect as you have given to others.

LADY IN PINK

Before anyone is requested to see anyone
Because of the color of their clothes
Or the color of their skin
It may be a pink petal of rose.

If one has security cameras
One must view it first
Never burden anyone that can cause them stress
'Cause you'll find thirst.
God can only quench the thirst
If we seek the truth first.

I'll admit being questioned
Because of the color of my clothes
Was very embarraessing
Which brought me many woes.

I haven't worne pink in a very long time
But now iI am hesitant to wear it again.
Pink is a pretty color
And in the end, the innocent will win.

Note: There was a black woman wearing pink at this apartment complex that got into a confrontation with a white female. The black female was searched for from the office, and because they saw me wearing pink, they called me in the office and questioned me in front of everyone which caused me total stress and embarrassment. I was appalling that they had cameras and didn't view it first. Instead they plucked the first black woman who had on pink into their office. This is profiling and it is not from God.

But since I had one of the best attorneys in America, Attorney Daniel J. Gauthier, attorney at law, he helped me get them off my back. If it wasn't for Dan Gauthier, I don't know what may have happened. This was illegal, and these people make their own rules of harassment, but they didn't know I had the best attorney there is. Mr. Gauthier is not a man one would want to reckon with in many areas in his life. He is a friend, and I am proud to say he is my attorney who has nothing but intelligence and knowledge for all his clients.

THE STAR

Looking up in the beautiful night sky,
there are a vast number of shining stars
twinkling and shining,
from beyond and afar.

Every twinkle differs,
but there is always one star
that captures your inner soul.
It is the calm and relaxing star.

The glowing and quiet stars are peaceful,
and each one is beautiful by itself,
but there is always one distinguishing star
that you keep on your shelf.

While drifting off to sleep,
while lying on the sand,
the last thing I remembered
was a star in the palm of my hand.

PLANT WHAT YOU NEED TO SOW

When a flower seed is planted,
it begins to grow
to a beautiful flower,
which you had to sow.

The warmth of the sun,
the rain from above,
nurture the seeds
that you planted with love.

When a marigold dies,
there are many seeds left inside
to be used for replanting,
once the seeds have dried.

Flowers blossom from May,
all through the summer,
for the beauty
and the sweet smell of myrrh.

CAPTURED HEART

I don't know what just happened to me.
One look in your eyes
and my heart was no longer free.
I think you've captured my heart.
I see you occasionally;
you always speak with a smile.
I said, "Let's take a walk."
Little did you know, I would have walked a mile.

The soft, puffy clouds began to grow dark.
The rain started to pour.
How nice the rain felt
as it began to rain more.

When you're in love,
the weather doesn't matter to you.
When you're in love,
no kind of weather makes you feel blue.

WEATHER THE STORM

Stand tall, firm, and steady,
just like the tree in a storm.
The branches sway this way and that way,
but it stands without harm.
Plant your roots on good and solid ground,
just like the tree, and steady you'll be.

After the storm, you hear only one sound.
The birds singing joyously
and a rainbow that's colorful and free.
The sun shining so bright,
lasting all the way 'til night.

Stand tall like the tree.
Let your light shine bright.
When you weather the storm,
you'll have better insight.

When the wind blows strong,
bend and don't break.
Do goodwill for all,
and God will never let you fall.

Sunshine always follows the storm.
Storms come and storms go.
Learn to weather them,
and beyond, you'll see the glow.

Plant your roots on good soil,
so when the storm does approach,
the roots won't wash away.
It just gets stronger every day.

God's blessings are abundant.
His grace is everlasting.
We thank you, dear Lord, for staying with us.
In Your name, we rejoice and sing.

EXCEL

Show love, patience, and kindness
throughout your everyday contact.
Listen before speaking,
before you begin to act.

Speak with tactfulness.
Be silent when listening.
Have an open mind and heart
before questioning.

No one is without flaw,
but we strive for our best.
Keep God in your heart,
and He will answer your request.

Share your knowledge, love, and understanding
with people in your everyday contact.
Encourage them to excel their potentials.
Give people hope, and start with their essentials.

Do not be judgmental
because we all have flaws.
Instead, lift their hearts and spirits,
and teach them God's laws.

After tonight has come and gone,
focus on using your skills.
Share them with others,
so they can learn to build.

HANG ON

When trouble seems to find you,
remember everything must pass.
Trouble may be present,
so hang on, and it will not last.

Don't mope or linger on negativity;
think positive, and that is where you'll head.
Cling attentively to what is right;
hang on in there, and don't be misled.

Good always overcomes anything bad.
Anything that is not good
will carry no weight.
But stand tall as you should.

Be patient for good things.
Have no tolerance for negativity.
Hang on in there,
and think positively.

MEN OF GOD

Men of God are blessed from the start.
They share among all
the good words of God
for you to stand tall and not fall.

Men of God are slow to anger.
They offer words of encouragement for all
to help you through tough times
when you come against a brick wall.

Men of God welcome you in.
They feed you with the truth
'til you hunger for more.
God's words are as sweet as a flute.

Men of God have great wisdom and knowledge
that no school could ever teach.
To be a student of God
brings you to be a man of God,
way beyond anyone's reach.

Blessed are those who hear the words of God,
and listen with both ears.
Blessed are the men of God
who teach you all through the years.

FRIENDSHIP

A friend is there at your door
just when you needed a friend.
A friend brings you lunch
just when you thought about food.
A friend listens when you're upset
just when you thought no one cared.
A friend called to say hello
just when you needed to talk.
A friend corrects you when you're wrong
just when you thought you were right.
A friend apologizes and admits when they're wrong.
A true friend accepts the apology.
A friend brings you a bowl of soup
because you were feeling ill.
A friend will help and not hinder
just when you needed a helping hand.
A friend is sent by God.
If you answer his knock, you will know.

A man who has friends must himself be friendly,
But there is a friend who sticks closer than a brother.
—Proverbs 18:24

SHARING

Stop, listen, and look around you.
What do you see?
Faces of your young and old,
sisters and brothers of all nationalities.

Some faces are sad,
full of despair.
Share your kindness
of how much God cares.

Lift each other up
when you see they need it most.
Join hands together
all nations and coast to coast.

Put the Lord in your life
to weather life's strife,
and He will never let you down.
Do goodwill for all,
and His Spirit will shine on you,
from town to town.

The only way is the right way.
There is a crooked road
and a straight road,
as it was once told.

Keep your eyes on the prize;
never let them wander.
Stabilize your eyes, and focus them.
Leave no areas for ponder.

Blessed be the man or woman
who selflessly gives his or her all.
All the money in the world is worth nothing.
It can't stand against His heavenly call.

MY LOVING GRANDCHILDREN

When my grandchildren were born,
the angels sang above.
My heart rejoiced,
and it was filled with love.

When I held them in my arms,
the angels sang above.
What a blessing they are,
my little turtledoves.

Their wide, beautiful smiles
always enlighten my day.
Their big, brown eyes are filled with joy
when they jump on the bales of hay.

They toddle and walk through the house
grabbing everything in sight,
examining every little object,
that they eventually try to bite.

Their fat, rosy cheeks have dimples
when they laugh and play.
Their little legs just keep on going
'til Granny retires for the day.

I love you with all my heart
and will guide, teach, and protect you.
I'll teach them how to fish,
and be there when they catch the big one too.

Today, you said your first word;
I was so proud of you.
We both clapped our hands
which encouraged them to say new words too.

I hold them in my arms when they're asleep
before settling them down in the bed to sleep.
I asked God to protect them, and watch over them
when I'm no longer here to hug them when they weep.

LIFE WITH ALZHEIMER'S

What are you thinking?
What are you trying to tell me?
How do you feel,
and tell me what you see?

You've lived a long and productive life.
You carried the world on your shoulders,
and not once did you complain.
You were always able to move boulders.

You provided for your family
and loved us unconditionally.
You were always there for us,
attending the children's rallies.

Every holiday, our table was a feast.
You smiled at your offspring
when it was time to eat.

When I look in your eyes, I see worry and pain.
How can I express to you we are all okay?
Your hard work was not in vain.

When I hold your hands, tears trimmed your eyes.
Please don't cry; I'm not saying goodbye.

I love you very much, and I will never leave you.
My heart cries out silently as well as yours does too.

But always remember this: just as sure as the sun rises
and just as sure as the sun sets;
I'll always love you no matter what the crisis.

A SISTER'S LOVE

A sister's love is like no other.
They're at your side when you need them.
You may have big arguments,
but they will always be your stem.

A stem is a part that supports another part.
It's also a line of ancestry.
The two are never apart; they are the mix of the same pastry.

STEPPING OUT OF DARKNESS

Before I came to know and love God,
I lived in a cocoon in the suburbs.
My life was neat and tidy in this cocoon.
How safe I felt in this cocoon.

When the cocoon opened,
I was blinded by the vast number of people.
I crawled back into my cocoon,
and the Lord said, "Come back out,
for you are My people."

At that time, I was shown a book,
a book of life, THE HOLY BIBLE.
So much knowledge and so much wisdom.
Everything you must know is in the Bible.

First, I read twenty pages of the Bible,
and it left me thinking.
I read fifty pages, and it left me bewildered.
I read four hundred pages, and it captured my soul.
I read one thousand pages, and I was drawn in
to the truth and everlasting life.

How beautiful and changed I had become.
All I had to do was open my heart
when I opened the Bible.

I left the cocoon to fly away.
To share the good news to anyone
who had two ears to listen.
I'm here to tell you that God listens,
loves, and protects us from our fears.
He'll make you fearless in all aspects.

To open blind eyes,
to bring out prisoners from the prison.
—Isaiah 42:7

TO FORGIVE

You may not be able to forget
but may be able to forgive.
In order to live life,
you have to forgive, in order to live.

To hold onto anger
means you have not forgiven.
You might not forget,
but you must forgive for a fulfillment of living.

FALLING DOWN

I fell and scraped my knees.
Please help me back to my feet?
God is surely watching you,
so please help me to my seat.

Help me brush off the dirt;
God will surely reward you.
My ankle is too weak to move.
One day, you may need my help too.

Never think twice about helping someone.
GOING ONCE! GOING TWICE!
Help is not an auction,
and it is not a game of dice.
Do goodwill for all,
and He will never let you fall.

Life is so great!
He blessed us with many gifts.
Grasp at it with all your heart.
Stand together and not apart.

For a righteous *man* may fall seven times,
And rise again,
But the wicked shall fall by calamity.
—Proverbs 24:16

THE HEART

The heart doesn't lie;
it holds the inner self of who you are.
You cannot be what you are not meant to be;
either it's of peace or it's of war.

If your heart is of peace,
it cannot make war;
especially if it shines like a golden fleece.

If your heart is of war,
you cannot find peace within yourself.
A chaotic heart leads to despair,
collecting dust upon a shelf.

Peace is of God and from God.
He'll plant seeds in your heart
that will not only benefit you
but others as well, right from the start.

When the heart is free, it grows constantly.
Doors begin to open widely.
As you look through the doors with awe,
with contentment you are where you were striving to be.

FOOLISH HEART

I could not see the real person;
I relied on my instincts.
My instincts were broadsided
by a foolish heart connected with chain links.

I loosened the tight links
that were braided with foolishness.
Fools will put themselves to shame
unwittingly, 'til you see why you were lame.

The Lord will enable you
to put your heart and mind
in the correct perspective.
Pray to Him not to leave you blind.

He answers all requests accordingly,
and He makes no mistakes.
All of His works are perfect.
He works while we are asleep and awake.

Once I was a fool, a fool indeed;
running with the blow of the leaves.
Never looking back for what was good;
now I look forward and know what to perceive.

The way of a fool *is* right in his own eyes,
But he who heeds counsel *is* wise.
A fool's wrath is known at once,
But a prudent *man* covers shame.
—Proverbs 12:15–16

PRIDE

Pride is a sorrowful thing to keep.
Having pride may prohibit you
from many blessings;
it keeps you from being new.
Pride is a person never admitting to be wrong,
even when they haven't a clue.

To have an abundance of pride
will eventually be your downfall.
It will keep you deaf;
you won't hear His heavenly call.

Pride *goes* before destruction,
And a haughty spirit before a fall.
Better *to be* of a humble spirit with the lowly,
Than to divide the spoil with the proud.
He who heeds the word wisely will find good.
                                    —Proverbs 16:18–20

TURN NEGATIVE TO POSITIVE

He was in a sad situation
and had to examine his living style.
He became angry at the way he was living,
for he had covered many grounds without a mile.

He slept wherever he could
through all types of weather.
He hadn't a dime in his pocket
nor a penny in his weather-beaten sweater.

He was a homeless man.
He lived on the streets and in parks every day
with hardly anything to eat.
He was adamant that changes would be made today.

He started to change his unfortunate situation
to something positive.
He opened his mind, heart, and soul
and discarded everything that was negative.

He made changes and applied for employment.
He excelled above all the other employees.
After six months, he was finally making a dent.

He turned something that was negative
and used that for an uplift
to turn it into something positive.

You have a heart, mind, and soul;
utilize all three to make one.
They are three in the same bowl,
all under the blessed sun.
With God, nothing is impossible.

PASS THE TORCH

A happy heart brings a warm smile.
A warm smile brings on a warmth of glow.
A warmth of glow brings serenity to others.
Serenity helps others grow.

Kind words bring a sense of ease to others.
Words of wisdom are better when shared.
Helping someone helps them to help others.
Show people that you care.
Show them that Jesus loves them as well.

DON'T GIVE UP

Reach far, climb high, and soar above.
Never give up on your dreams.
Work at it diligently;
things are not as hard as they seem.

Live your life to its fullest extent.
Continue to excel;
don't give up.
Hold on, and life will treat you well.

No need for pondering on things that were meant to be.
Instead, concentrate on the next phase.
Cling to your strategy;
do not succumb to a haze.

Put one foot in front of the other;
continue to walk ahead without stumbling.
Good, strong, sturdy strides are of confidence,
and steadiness brings on wings.

Don't give up.
Think negative, and that is where you will stay.
Think positive, and it will take you a long way.

Fly like the eagle, and soar with precision.
Strong, sturdy wings are very graceful.
Don't give up.
Being positive is very delightful.

DREAMS AND GOALS

It's amazing how we work at something
diligently and relentlessly.
Then one day, you take notice
of what you've done daily.

Then everything pays off, because you've
been steadfast in your good ways.
Be patient for your expected outcome;
it will be the joy of your days.

Put your heart into your dreams.
Put your mind on your goals,
and never give up hope
because hope strengthens the soul.

God will work with you when your good works are seen.
Have an open mind and heart,
and the rest will flow like the stream.

The stream is a beautiful sight;
the water is perfect and clear.
Believe in yourself,
and what was far was always near.

A BREAKFAST PRAYER IN SEPTEMBER 2001 "WE WILL NEVER FORGET"

There is nothing more important than family and friends
sharing time together and eating together.
To have time for each other
no matter the season or the weather.

We thank you, dear Lord Jesus Christ,
for giving us this day
to spend together
and hear us as we pray.

We ask You, dear Lord,
to continue to bless our friends and family every day.
We ask for strength and guidance
and to mold us Your way.

We pray for the victims of the terrorist attacks,
their families, and the rescue workers too.
We pray for our president and his officials,
for their decisions that affect the old and the new.

We pray for our parents and loved ones
who have joined You in the past.
We thank you for opening doors,
for you are the first and the last.
You are the Alpha and the Omega
who loves us no matter what our flaws may be.
You are the roots of our tree.

Keep us with You, dear Lord;
never let us go.
Without your light,
there will never be a glow.

The light of life,
You've blessed us with indeed.
Keep our families under Your dome.
For today, we have planted a seed;
a seed that will sprout and grow
to a beautiful flower,
in which we had to sow.

AN AWAKENING DREAM

Once I had a dream,
a dream that felt like it was real,
and when I had awakened
my world stood still.

I dreamed of my mother
wearing a black dress, with long sleeves,
with one bold white stripe.
I heard the rustling of leaves.

My mother was lying down
as tears filled my eyes.
Then I realized that she had passed.
I looked up in the heavenly skies.

Asking God, "Why?"
My heart was very saddened.
I never said goodbye.

The dream had disturbed me.
Dreams come and dreams go.
The dream eventually left my thoughts;
my spirits were no longer low.

As weeks went on, my mom did pass away.
Suddenly, the dream had returned to me.
I knew then, God was preparing me;
preparing me for what was going to be.

My siblings and I miss Mom dearly.
We found peace among each other.
God had brought our family together,
with all the sisters and brothers.

How strange it is for sisters and brothers
to live in the same town
and yet not really visit each other,
until something sits them down.

Love one another; never take life in haste
because you may look back one day
and think, *What a waste.*

JUDGING AND TRUTHFULNESS

How quick we are to judge,
never looking at both sides.
"'Judgment is Mine,' says the Lord."
With these words we must abide.

It's so easy to turn away from the truth;
to refuse to be involved with what is right.
Please never forget,
only a coward takes flight.

Never run from the truth;
the truth will surely override a lie.
Stand fast for what is right;
with the truth, there are no questions why.

The aftermath of a lie
is sure to ruin you.
Be truthful and honest,
and your days will never be blue.

Do not stand rigid.
Have courage to tell the truth,
even if it means the risk of losing.
Just remember the book of Ruth.

LIFE WITH YOU

Life is better when it's shared.
All your days are brighter
just knowing someone cares.

To have someone to share breakfast with,
and assist each other preparing lunch.
Taking walks together and listening to the leaves crunch.

When you're in love, everything has a silver lining.
Even when it rains,
the sun remains shining.

I thank God for sending you into my life.
I thank God for making me your loving wife.

CARING

Speak softly when speaking;
don't raise your voice needlessly.
Treat everyone with respect.
You may need that person you see.

Listen when spoken to;
don't speak in haste.
Listen attentively;
to listen inattentively may be a waste.

If you're asked to help,
don't turn the other way.
You just may need
that same person one day.

What I am telling you
is very plain and simple.
Treat people and your surroundings with care,
and you'll never have a scratch or a pimple.
You'll be blemish-free and shine through the crowd.
You'll find favor from the Lord,
when He calls your name out loud.

AN ETHIOPIAN WEDDING

Watching the video
does no justice
for the beauty and grace
of the Ethiopian race.

Their singing is music for the soul.
Peaceful, joyous, and free,
all mixed in a bowl.

The clothes are divine,
sewn with love in each thread.
Swaying in the wind,
and beautiful dress wears for the head.

As the vows were exchanged,
two hearts became one
to live in harmony,
under the sun.

GOD IS WITH US

I see you looking out the window every day,
gazing constantly and barely blinking.
Your tone of voice is kind and low.
I often wonder what you're thinking.

Although you acknowledge my presence,
you're still very distant from your surroundings.
Would you like some coffee or something to eat?
Tell me, what would you like me to bring?

Would you like me to comb you hair,
or would you like to talk?
I'm a good listener,
or maybe we could take a walk.

Tears trimmed your eyes
when I hugged you today.
Tell me, what's wrong?
You said, "Let's pray."

Your prayer began with tears and sobs.
I held your hands; you prayed with a song.
You looked me in the eyes and said,
"Why do I have Alzheimer's? What did I do wrong?"

You did nothing wrong, my dear.
Some things are meant for us to know,
and some things remain a mystery.
But let me tell you that Jesus shows in your glow.

We must count our blessings
and not forget the blessings that are in store.
God sent us into your life to help you,
and He has opened many doors.

So please don't think you are forgotten.
He will never leave us.
God sent His only son, Jesus,
to walk among us.
He sent this entire staff to be with you
to meet all your needs,
and we love you too.

VALUE A TRUE FRIEND

Friendship is a valued bond,
that is a blessing to treasure.
If you've found a true friend,
it is something to treasure forever.

Being a true and honest friend
works both ways, you see.
If you should happen to cross a friend,
sail yourself out to sea.
Don't bother to throw in the anchor
to stop sailing the boat.
Your trust has been broken forever;
now you must learn to float.

If you break a friend's trust,
then you were not a true friend from the start.
There was already a seed planted within you,
buried deep in your heart.

If dishonesty is in you
and your friend is unaware of it,
have grace and decency to walk away.
Don't fall into the dark pit.

But if you are to be a true friend,
pray for God to stay in your midst.
Because without Him by your side,
things can take a twist.

SHARE THE LIGHT

Prosperity is gained when it is earned.
It is continuous for all your days,
given by the grace of God,
because you're steadfast in your good ways.

Share your prosperity;
don't misuse or abuse it.
Even if you only help one person,
this is a candle you have lit.

Keep your candle burning, so the light won't burn out.
To be in the dark is a losing bout.

Share the candle so that others can see.
Show them the light; the rest will come naturally.

MOM

My mother was a strong woman,
a woman who has seen a lot.
She was also an excellent mom;
there was always food in the pot.

Sometimes it's hard to write about Mom;
I guess because I miss her so much.
My mom passed away years ago;
I do miss her motherly touch.

We shared tears and laughs.
We shared good and bad times.
We had good times on the front porch
listening to the wind chimes.

When I feel low in spirits,
I remember her wise conversations we shared.
My heart cries out
when I think of how much she cared.

Dear Mom, I love you dearly.
I love you with all of my heart.
Continue to pray for me, Mom;
you've been my rock from the start.

You wiped my tears away
whenever I cried.
You always knew when I was truthful,
and you knew when I lied.

You chased away bullies
when I was in grammar school.
You were always there;
you taught me the golden rule.
You were present to guide me
all through my teenage years.
When I was scared,
you chased away my fears.

How can I thank you
for giving me the breath of life?
But most importantly, I thank you
for teaching me to deal with life's strife.

COMING TOGETHER

Come, all nations, together;
let's talk togetherness, peace, and unity.
There is no need for disputes;
let's hold hands from now to eternity.

Let's slice bread at the same table.
Let's eat and talk peace, you see.
Let's share our thoughts,
and let our minds be free.

Life was meant to be joyous;
life was not meant to be chaotic.
Enjoy life, treasure it, and grasp at it.
Don't wait for the end of the wick;
the candle is burning,
melting within a matter of hours,
while the world is turning.

Come, all nations; let's adhere to each other.
Communication is all we need.
I know we can do it
with God's help indeed.

We are all God's children,
and we need to come to an agreement under God's laws.
Your heart will surely be gladdened.
He made the world without flaw.

MISTAKES

Mistakes can happen to anyone.
You can learn from mistakes you make
by not doing them twice.
This is good advice to take.

Mistakes are not meant to torment you;
they are meant to teach you,
or they can make you a better person.
They can bring you from old to new.

You can teach others from your mistakes,
or you can even build from them.
Pondering on mistakes
may plunge your wits.

Stay sharp and focused; teach others what you've learned.
This may prevent others from taking the wrong turn.

LET GOD FIGHT YOUR BATTLES

You have tried to slander my name, and you failed.
Instead, you put yourself to shame.
You tried to throw daggers at me, and you failed.
Instead, you tripped over the daggers.
You tried to destroy my livelihood, and you failed.
Nothing you do will come of any good.
You tried to take away my possessions, and you failed.
Instead, you lost your only possession.
You tried to tear down anything I built, and you failed.
You have no heart and felt no guilt.
You tried to spread rumors about me, and you failed.
I have truth that will follow me.
Everything you tried to do to me always failed
because God fights my battles for me.

Whoever hides hatred *has* lying lips,
And whoever spreads slander *is* a fool.
—Proverbs 10:18

CHILDREN OF GOD

Children of God
will share His kingdom in heaven.
They are blessed from the start,
every sister and all the brethren.

Children of God
welcome you in.
They share bread and butter
as if you were kin.

Children of God
share words of goodwill.
They are apt to hear the good words.
You are fed to your fill.

Children of God
are known to mankind.
The glow is noticed immediately.
If you seek, you will find
the kindness that is within.

Your cupboard is never bare
once your shelves are clear,
and you've made room for what is in store;
then you discover it was always near.

A CHRISTMAS DINNER PRAYER

To our family and friends,
We would like to wish everyone a merry Christmas,
as we celebrate Jesus's birthday tonight.

Tomorrow is not promised to us,
but God has promised this day to us.
We thank you, dear Lord,
because in God we trust.

I look at Mom's offspring,
as we stand before Him.
What a wonderful blessing He's given us.
He fills our cup to the rim.

We thank you, dear Lord, for your leniency,
because we all have flaws.
Not one of us is perfect.
We will teach our offspring Your Laws.

My heart is happy
for all Your blessings, that You gave us here.
We praise and thank Jesus
for all our blessings this year.

I turn my attention to the younger members of the family.
Listen, learn, observe, and record.
Tomorrow is not promised to us.
It is time to open your door.

One day, soon, you will head the family
and bring everyone together every year.
When He calls your name, you will know.
It will be a blessing, and you will have nothing to fear.

He makes no mistakes;
His plans are always with perfection.
Listen to Him, and learn from Him.
He hears all confessions.

In Jesus name, let us hold hands as we pray His prayer:
the OUR FATHER.

THANKS TO AN INSTRUCTOR

I've met many people, here and abroad,
but one particular person stands out in the crowd.
Her outlook was honest and fair.
She stood tall and proud.

I met her in nursing school;
she helped me more than she knows.
I listened to her for a year,
as I sat in the back row.

I'll never forget her stamina and teachings.
She was never judgmental.
Her door was always open for personal meetings.
Her language and teaching were of leadership tone.

Three times, I thought of quitting,
but I decided to stay and fight for what was right.
She exhibited commitment to teaching us.
She always stood for what was right.

She was making and molding us
to be professional nurses in our field.
We learned critical thinking.
From her, we learned to build.

I find myself using everything she taught us
in my nursing field, to this day.

I personally learned to be a strong nurse
and to use my skills in every way.

VALUED FRIENDSHIP

A personality everyone strives for and a heart as warm as a fireplace.
Her fairness is real; she sees people as they are.
She does not differentiate with any race.

She is fair and honest.
She cares for human life.
A nurse that's very knowledgeable, to deal with any strife.

Friends are in many categories, but this friend is in my corner.
Through any situation, she's a teacher, not a scorner.

Friends come and friends go; true friendship stays 'til the end.
Cherish these types of friends because they are heaven-sent.

BE ATTENTIVE

The house was filled with faint smoke;
dark smoke was beneath one door.
I ran to find my family
as I crawled low on the floor.

Everyone was outside
except for one family member.
I ran back into the house and searched.
Then I remembered.
She can't possibly be in that room
where the dark smoke was coming from beneath the door.
I ran toward the room
and held my breath once more.

I was blinded by smoke,
and I could not possibly enter the room.
I ran back outside to look for her again.
My heart felt nothing but gloom.

While I was crying, I heard a distant telephone ring.
That's when I realized that it was only a dream.

The dream puzzled me, and I asked God, *What did it mean?*
My answer was it was difficult for me to enter the room.
I could not find the one I loved,
and it gave me a feeling of gloom.
My heart was saddened in this dream.
God is saddened when we don't let Him in,
and then we are lost from Him.

This was an awakening dream
that I began to take heed to,
and I realized that Jesus was knocking.
He wanted to bring me from old to new.

LOOK AT THE WHOLE PICTURE

I once had a conversation with a man,
who told me there is no need
to help anyone with a bad attitude.
I told him he must learn to lead.

He argued that he was right
which led me to tell him
a true story, to show him the light,
to bring him out of the dim.

There was an employee
whose attitude in life was negative.
Every day, she was angry
and never thought positive.

She always had an argument
and did not care what she said.
The nurse who was her supervisor
observed her from toe to head.

Her shoes were worn down;
she walked with pain in every step she took.
The nurse examined the size of her feet
and gave it a second look.

The nurse realized she wore size eight.
The next day, she brought her a pair
of tennis shoes,
to show her someone cared.

The nurse told her, she hoped she didn't mind,
but she bought these shoes and they did not fit;
would she please accept these shoes
as an early Christmas gift?

The employee took the shoes
and said, "It is a perfect fit."
She hugged the nurse and thanked her.
A candle was then lit.

One week later, the employee
turned into a model staff member.
Her bad attitude no longer existed.
It was Christmas in November.

MARRIAGE AND TRUST

Marriage is a cherished partnership.
Trust is what adheres a marriage together.
You must trust each other,
not just sometimes, but forever.

If trust is ever broken
between a woman and a man,
it shatters a relationship
that will no longer stand.

You cannot have harmony without trust.
Distrust leads to chaos in the home
until eventually, one day,
you're all alone.

Think about the consequences
that may occur before you commit a distrustful act,
or you may ruin your relationship,
and that's a fact.

If your mind tells you it's wrong
and your heart steers you astray,
put your mind and heart together;
this will lead you the right way.

A PROPOSAL

There was a couple eating dinner.
The man looked his companion in the eyes
and told her that he picked a winner.

Along came a waiter holding a silver platter.
The man got down on one knee, and his companion was flattered.

The waiter removed the silver lid and revealed a velvet ring case.
You should have seen the look on her face.
He opened the case that held a diamond ring.
Little did she know, he was about to sing.
Of course, she accepted his marriage proposal
as everyone clapped loudly.
The man kissed her so proudly.

GIVE WITH YOUR HEART

It's amazing how we take things for granted.
We walk by a homeless person and drop him a dollar.
We walk away feeling that we've done our duty,
the cold wind brushing up against our collar.

Have you ever thought maybe that person has a name?
Next time ask him when you pass him by.
Maybe we could ask him would he like a cup of coffee.
Or maybe we could call a shelter before we pass him by.

Maybe we could bring him a warm pair of socks
or even a warm wool sweater,
ask him if he has family,
or even talk about the weather.

When I was seven years old, I was walking by Union Station
with two of my older sisters one day.
We passed a homeless man who asked us for change.
My sister said, "We have no change today."

As we walked on by, I turned back to observe the man,
and he was eating orange peelings out of a waste can.
I started crying and begged my sisters;
"Can we please give him our bus fare?
Could we walk so the man can eat?
Please," I said, "We just have to care."

My sisters gave me their change
and said, "Here, go give it to him before he eats more peelings."
The man took the change, and I wondered what was he feeling.
My sisters yelled for me to come back to them.
She said, "Here is more change; go give it to him."

I ran to give him more change, and the man smiled and said, "No,"
that we had given him plenty.
He said, "God bless you," as he tapped my head and told me to go.

I told my sisters he refused the other change.
We took our eyes away from him,
for not more than two seconds, and he was gone.
My sister said, "It might have been Him."
I asked her, "Who is Him?"
She said, "God. He might have been an angel from God."
To this day, with grandchildren of my own now,
I still think of the man I met by Union Station
whenever I read "Footprints in the Sand."

A LEADER FROM GOD

I often think of Dr. Martin Luther King Jr.
I wish I could have met him.
He was sent from God to lead us.
His cup was blessed to the rim.

He spoke of peace, love, and unity.
He was against violence too.
He fought with all of his heart and soul
and prayed when he was feeling blue.

He prayed for everyone and loved God with all his heart.
Blessed abundantly by God, he was the chosen from the start.

His voice was of wisdom, truth, and knowledge.
His eyes were the sincerity and love.
His knowledge was beyond anyone's reach.
Light shined on him from up above.

He preached to anyone who would listen.
Those with one ear turned away.
Those with both ears did not go astray.

He walked endlessly for freedom informing
the world of "THE DREAM."
The dream of what God had shown him, with his eyes full of gleam.

May God continue to bless his family
and pour everlasting grace on them as well.
We thank God for his family too,
as we listen to the freedom bell.

WISDOM GAINED

Your sincerity is genuine, and your mannerism is exquisite.
Your vocabulary is knowledge heard, and your words are definite.

Your respect was earned dutifully with the
words of wisdom you spoke.
Each word had a significant stroke.

Continue to learn as you grow.
Leave no room for chaos in your midst.
Think before you speak
because your name is already on the good list.

MARTIN LUTHER KING JR.:
A MAN OF HONOR

A man of leadership and honor.
A man of God who was sent to teach us
about truth and unity.
A man we could trust.

God was his strength
and the fire within him.
He walked many miles
and sometimes singing hymns.

His name was Dr. Martin Luther King Jr.
A man sent to lead and guide us.
A man of justice.

He walked many roads, tirelessly and consistently, every day.
He was about his Father's business,
to show us the way.

Sometimes he walked or rode the bus,
spreading truth, light, and justice for all.
He was a man of integrity, who tumbled down many walls.

He was sent by Jesus to bring messages for us to know.
He never took a seat at the back of the row.
He was always up front, marching endlessly, for everyone
under the heavenly sun.

FRIENDS

Many years have gone by since we first met.
I just wanted to say thank you
for being one of the best.

You've been like a brother.
An inspiration you always are.
I just wanted to say I love you.
You have a heart that shines like a star.
You're like the brother I've always wanted,
but then again you are;
because we are all sisters and brothers in God,
whether near or far.

JEALOUSY

Jealousy is hard to hide.
You may try to disguise it with a veil
by trying to cover it up
but eventually, even that will fail.

Jealousy will blend through your appearance.
The blind will see it with their eyes.
Sooner or later, it will become evident
and become more difficult to hide.

Jealousy has existed from the beginning of time.
One must distinguish within themselves
the good from the bad,
keeping the dust off your shelf.

Letting clutter or dust collect
on anything that should be dust-free
will eventually build and build,
right up to your knees.

Jealousy makes a person very distrustful.
They will swallow themselves in hate
because jealousy burdens one's heart.
They hurry themselves to a desolate fate.

Even the deaf can hear the words of the jealous at heart.
Their words are unkind and distasteful, of sour tart.

Jealousy is obvious if you look at it.
You can see it through a stack of madras with your eyes.
From a mouth of lies,
jealousy has destroyed many lives.

Disassociate yourself from people with jealousy in their heart.
They will squeeze your goodness from you, right from the start.

Flee from distrustful surroundings.
Adhere yourself to positive things in life.
Keep faith in the Lord,
to deal with life's strife.

LOVE DEFINED

Love is defined as a strong affection
or a warm attachment.
It can be so strong
that it makes you feel commitment.

Love is also an attraction
based on sexual desires.
It warms your heart.
It can feel like a burning fire.

Then there's lovelorn,
being deprived of love.
When the fire dies out,
you throw in the glove.

Love is a funny thing.
It can make you happy
or blind you,
to where you can't see.

Love can make you sad
'til all your days feel blue,
or it can make you feel complete,
or feel like a fool.

Love can bring good times
and bad times.
It can bring you sorrow
or make you hear wind chimes.

One thing for sure;
love plays an important role
in everyone's lives.
It can make you rich or pay a toll.

Only you can decide
how to treasure love in your life.
Handle it with care,
or it can bring you strife.

HIDDEN VOICE

My life is in your hands;
I'm fragile at my age.
I feel like a bird
locked inside a cage.
I spread my wings to fly,
but there is nowhere to go.
Therefore, you are my sole caregiver;
your wings carry me a flow.

You are my voice
because I am unable to speak.
I depend on you every day,
sometimes week to week.

You are my legs
when you transfer me
from wheelchair to bed.
You are the roots, and I am the tree.

You are my hands
when it is time to eat.
Look at my eyes;
I'm longing for that piece of meat.

You are my strength;
I depend on you for all my needs.
Examine my body language;
please dress me up in those pretty beads.

You are the caregivers
who help me when I'm ill.
You nourish me back to health,
and get me over the hill.

I am the raft in the sea;
you are the ores
that glide me to shore
and protect me from the tides that roar.

I am the voice that you do not hear;
I speak with my eyes
and sometimes through my tears.

GOD IS JUDGE OVER ALL

Some are quick to judge other people without even knowing them.
The quick to judge lives are usually grim.

Their lives are miserable.
They talk badly about beautiful people they do or don't know
because they can find no wrong in the right.
They prohibit themselves to grow.

They're stuck in a ditch and don't know how to step out.
Instead, they stay there where they can grope and pout.

They see beauty in the ugly
and hate anything that has righteous beauty.
Their thinking is usually backwards.
Being angry and deceitful is their duty.

One good potato is better than a bag of rotten ones to eat.
With one good potato, you have a choice
of mashed, fried, or baked over heat.
No one has any use for a bag of rotten potatoes.
They are discarded where the rest of the garbage goes.

SORROW

He was the firstborn son;
a son who had grown to be a man.
He respected everyone except for his number one fan.

His mom was proud of him, from birth to a man.
His only mother whom he thought he was better than.

His friends all smiled and laughed in his face;
all the time thinking he was a disgrace to the human race
because he disrespected the only one in the world
who gave him birth
and raised him here on earth.

His mom passed away;
then he realized he was all alone,
and no one else really cared.
He was a dog without a bone.

A wise son makes a glad father,
But a foolish son *is* the grief of his mother.
—Proverbs 10:1

GOD DELIVERS

I listened to a man
tell a true story one day.
He said he was about to be lynched,
and it was doomsday.

He told the story
about a mob of angry men
who had accosted him to the nearest tree,
where he remembered all his sins.

He told the story as if you could see it yourself.
He shouted to the men, "I'm innocent. Please let me go!"
No, they said, "You're guilty,
and this we know!"

He pleaded for them to free him,
and they would not listen at all.
They looped the rope around his neck;
then, they heard a call.

The voice came from up above saying,
"LET THAT MAN GO! HE HAS DONE NO WRONG!"
Everyone stood still,
and the silence was long.
The crowd of angry men became docile,
and they dropped the rope and walked away.
The man dropped to his knees
and began to pray.

This is actually a true story;
the man that told it is alive today.
He told everyone with two ears
that they should learn how to pray.

To hear the voice of the Lord,
we must all take heed.
His will be done,
and the Bible we must read.

That if you confess with your mouth the Lord Jesus and believe in your heart that God has raised him from the dead, you will be saved. For with the heart one believes unto righteousness, and with the mouth confession is made unto salvation. For the scripture says, "Whoever believes on Him will not be put to shame."

—Romans 10:9–11

THANK YOU, JESUS, FOR
CARING NURSES

We sometimes get caught up in the rush of life;
then days turn into months and years.
Not even stopping to smell the flowers blossom
or to hug someone that sheds a tear.

We get so busy with our routines.
Maybe we should take a day and make it a holiday or every day.
A holiday where we bind together and pray.

Or maybe we could thank our coworkers for
being a gem and working as a team.
Sometimes I wonder why we can't see the light for the beam.

God has His way of getting people together.
If He willed it, then there's a reason for it.
Thank Him for opening our eyes and keeping the candle lit.

Once God has kindled the fire in your heart, it never burns out.
Even if you think it has, make no mistake,
God will never lose a bout.

Continue to help others, and share your knowledge
with people in your everyday contact you meet.
God has an abundance of blessings for you
so that the cold will feel like heat.

THE REASON MAY NOT BE SEEN

There's a reason for everything that occurs.
It may be good,
or it may be bad.
Then, it's understood.

There's a reason why you made a left instead of a right.
The wrong or the left turn may have saved your life that night.
There's a reason why you stayed home today.
There may have been someone to lead you astray.

There's a reason for everything in your life.
You have a heart, mind, and soul.
Take heed to all three;
they are three in one bowl.

Now faith is the substance of things hoped
for, the evidence of things not seen.
—Hebrews 11:1

A TRIBUTE TO PATTON

He stood over six feet tall.
His courage and wisdom were great.
He was a chosen leader
and was never late.

His heart was a sea of courage.
His mind was conditioned to winning wars.
His intelligence was known worldwide
as he battled under the glistening stars.

He led his men to combat,
fighting right by their side.
A general with three stars
and a Bible by his side worldwide.

He prayed on his knees
for victory and good weather throughout the war.
The men were confused,
but prayed as they walked afar.

His name was General George S. Patton.
A man of honor, dignity, and knowledge.
A great war hero
who attended West Point Military College.

He foretold the coming of future events;
he knew the past as the future.
He was also a magnificent writer
who never came apart at the sutures.

All his victories were prosperous;
he knew this from the beginning.
Ignoring man's military orders,
he was adamant on winning.

He died of complications from an accident
after the war was over and won.
He fulfilled his destiny
after all was said and done.

THE LION

She walked through the forest
picking fruits and leafy vegetables.
A delightful basket
full of eatables.

A beautiful hand-carved bow and arrow
pressed against her flank.
Walking cautiously through the woods
as her heart began to sink.

A lion stared deep within her eyes.
She slowly lowered the basket down.
Sliding out her bow and arrow
while backing up toward her town.

As she tripped over a pile of rocks,
she withdrew her ivory knife.
She pierced the lion several times.
With the help of the Lord, this saved her life.

She made a net out of twigs and vines
and carried the dead lion back to town,
displaying her victory
to all the people around.

"Listen!" she shouted. "I was gathering food,
and along came this lion to end my life,
but I killed him instead
with my ivory knife."

"Praise God!" she shouted.
"I'm alive and here to tell you;
just have a little faith,
and God will save you too."

DISCIPLINE

Self-discipline comes from within you.
It comes from knowledge and wisdom gained.
It protects you from many unpleasant things
and informs you when to refrain.

Lack of discipline is for the undecided.
Teach them what is gained with self-discipline.
Continue to teach the young and old alike,
and you will win between the thin lines within.

Teach your generation of family values,
and bring wonders of good to them.
They will learn to appreciate and replicate themselves
of the gem within.

Life is an everlasting teaching process
for others and ourselves as well.
You must teach, talk, and demonstrate;
then take them to drink from the well.
The well of wisdom, truth, discipline,
love, and the opening of the eyes.
The well of life and God's words,
for this is imperative to our lives.

DEDICATION

Dedication is a strong inner drive
that outweighs the negative obstacles of your surroundings.
Some may find your drive
to be astronomically astounding.
Everyone has that sort of drive,
to be dedicated to something they believe in,
but to adhere to dedication
you must strive to overcome and win.

If you're not dedicated to what you desire,
do not proceed to grasp at it.
To pursue something you really don't desire
will only lead to forfeit.
Education may be your desire;
choose a field, and be dedicated to it.
Do your best at what you decide.
Dedicate yourself, and do not quit.

Once you have devoted and dedicated yourself
toward anything in life,
you must continue to educate yourself
to deal with any strife.
Once your mind is made up, you will definitely know.
You'll constantly work at it as you continue to grow.

THE MAN IN THE SHACK

There once was a man who suffered much pain and sorrow.
He knew of hardship and heartache.
He left his land behind
for the goodness of his own sake.

He came upon a new town
where he found a vacant and unclaimed
abandoned shack.
Somewhere no one knew his name.

He worked and cleaned up his shack,
for this was now his home.
His heart was gladdened
because he no longer had to roam.

Little did he know the hardships
that would soon be knocking at his door.
The neighbors took a dislike to him
and talked about the clothes he wore.
They hated him for no reason.

He suffered mental and physical abuse from the town's people.
He ignored them all and walked with his head high.
But he cried every night when he prayed
because he was afraid that he was going to die.

The Lord heard his cries
and sent a group of people to his defense.
The defense team worked diligently,
uncovering the town's pretense.

The man that once lived in the shack
was awarded thousands of dollars.
He now lives in the suburbs
with a vast amount of white collars.

What you have just read
actually occurred in our lifetime.
Keep your faith, and never give up,
for every passing there is a time.

THE GOOD AND THE BAD

How sad and lonely some people are. The sad get sadder,
the lonely get lonelier, and the mad get madder.
Their hearts are full of hate, drowned in despair,
trying hard to spread gloom because they just don't care.
These poor souls are lost and not aware of it;
make no mistake, they're digging their own pit.
Misery is fruitful with its own company;
they will pull you down to the river.
Sorrow is their joy;
it will make you quiver.

Mix with your equals who are delightful.
Hang onto their coattails, and enjoy the breeze from the ride.
Refresh yourself from the well, and wait for the tide.
Depart yourself from the miserable,
and make your presence scarce with hateful people.
Run toward the good of life;
you will find it at the top of the steeple.

Soar toward the positive things in life,
and adhere to what is right.
You'll have no regrets, and all of your burdens will be light.

HARD TIMES

He spent thirty-seven years in jail and thirty-seven years of thinking,
lying awake at night, and barely sleeping.
He was sorry for committing a crime,
and there was no way out until he did his time.
He took one day at a time and tried to
forget his family he loved dearly.
Angry that he may never see them again,
for he was not thinking clearly.

He started listening to the radio and watching religious programs.
His heart began to soften when he read a telegram.
The telegram read, his death sentence was pardoned.
He walked away from death row.
His heart was no longer hardened.

In his new cell, he dropped to his knees right away,
thanking God for his life and allowing him to see another day.

He was free to go after thirty-seven years,
and he vowed never to return to jail
because he was now aware
of the difference between heaven and hell.

This is actually a true story.
If you ask God for forgiveness of sin, with all of your heart and soul,
He remembers it no more.

FAMILY REUNION UNITES

Family reunions are important to have;
it brings families together yearly.
It's a day of celebration,
when you see everything clearly.

The children running and playing
with food clutched in their hands.
Children falling down and laughing
into the box of sand.

Families remembering all the good times
they had when they were young,
laughing, joking, and dancing under the hot sun.
The smell of hickory smoke fills the air;
your stomach longing for food as it growls like a bear.

Twelve long and short hours of having fun
with your family in the park
soon comes to an end when it gets dark.
Thank You, God, for our families and the joy of life with them.
He blessed our cups right to the rim.

PILLAR OF STRENGTH

She worked all her life, long hours every day,
just to feed her family because her husband had gone astray.
She had seven children that she raised all alone,
not once complaining, while working her fingers to the bone.

She always had plenty for her children to eat;
her cupboard was never bare.
The children never had to walk;
they always had bus fare.

She lived to see the majority of her grandchildren.
She never remarried.
Her husband left her years ago,
with the burden of the world to carry.

Come to Me, all *you* who labor and are heavy laden, and I will give
you rest. Take My yoke upon you and learn from Me, for I am
gentle and lowly in heart, and you will find rest for your souls.
For My yoke *is* easy and My burden is light.
—Matthew 11:28–30

A FRIEND SENT AND NOTHING GAINED

Cathy was in need of everything.
Her husband did not allow her to have friends.
He did not allow her to work,
and he refused helping hands.

Her electricity was due for disconnect.
She had three children to worry about.
The Lord sent her a friend
who carried a lot of clout.

The heaven-sent friend had little money
but carried much knowledge.
She was sent to help the family learn how
to attend the wisdom college.
Cathy listened and learned, and she was
able to overcome her hardships.
She escalated by exercising knowledgeable tips.

Cathy soon became envious of her heaven-sent friend.
She turned her back on the only one who
had a helping hand to lend.
The heaven-sent friend went on her way to help others in need.
Cathy's life went back downhill because she failed to take heed.

STRONG DESIRES

Her heart was driven from memories of what could be.
The drive in her heart
put her goals into gear.
This was the beginning of a new start.

She chose to escalate in various fields
because she had the love and desire
to do them all,
until it was time for her to retire.

All her works were for people as this is what she was destined to do.
She found that to love what you do keeps everything brand-new.
Her will came from a seed planted within her from birth.
God had chosen her to help others for her time here on earth.

Her death was peaceful and quiet
as her family sat by her side.
Her last words were, "Jesus, save me,"
and He opened His arms wide.

TO A DIRECTOR OF NURSING
(THIS POEM IS DEDICATED)

I met her about sixteen years ago.
Then our paths crossed again by fate, as
she rushed onto the elevator to avoid being late.

After sixteen years, she hadn't aged at all;
her outstanding demeanor still glowed.
A professional and intelligent nurse
reaping the good she had sowed.

I smiled at her and thanked her
for all the encouragement she had given me.
The seed that she had planted
had sprouted limbs from the tree.

She was now our director of nursing,
and it was her first day.
I was happy to know we had a leader
who would work with us in every way.

I told her that I was now a licensed nurse,
and she had inspired others and me years ago.
Her supervision was like no other nurse.
She taught us what we needed to know.

She was always teaching and helping others.
These qualities are a must, in our field.
A beautiful person with a heart of gold,
from her, we learned to build.

To this day, she doesn't know
how many people she helped, along the way.
She never slighted anyone.
I sincerely thank her, to this day.

It is a must, to treat everyone with respect
because you never know whose path you may cross, from the past.
Always keep in mind that your first impression
might also be your last.

"For the mountains shall depart
And the hills be removed,
But My kindness shall not depart from you
Nor shall my covenant of peace be removed,"
Says the LORD who has mercy on you.
—Isaiah 54:10

YOUR ACTIONS

Be careful of your actions in life.
You may not care what you do at one time
but, sooner or later, your actions can make you walk the line.

Be careful what you say in life.
You may not care what you say at one time
but, sooner or later, your words can make you blind.

Be careful whose shoes you step on.
You may not care whose shoes they are,
but they may be an army of shoes that refuses peace and makes war.

Be careful of the heart you may break.
You may look back one day
and decide you made a mistake.
But then, your true love has gone astray.

Be careful what you do, and be careful what you say
because you just may need that same person one day.

EYES WIDE OPEN

You're looking at a reflection,
not really seeing the real thing.
Look beyond the reflection,
and accept what it brings.

Life sometimes brings you lessons
that no school could ever teach.
Experience bring forth wings
way beyond anyone's reach.

Eyes wide closed seeing what your heart desires.
Eyes wide open seeing beyond the blue skies.

The heart can sometimes mislead you;
therefore, listen to your inner soul.
Keep your eyes open as life unfolds.

Grasp at life with all its pleasures,
and it will treat you well.
Enjoy life's treasures,
and listen to the freedom bell.

BUT HILLY'S SPIRIT REMAINED HIGH WITH CONSISTENCY

Hilly was hired at another company
and became an excellent nurse in her field.
Past negativity from Dee
made her strong, and she learned to build.

Five years had passed, and their paths crossed again.
Hilly had already established clout.
Dee was distraught when she saw Hilly's face.
Dee saw that she had started a losing bout.

Later that year, Dee was charged with patient abuse,
and some of her patients died.
What came out of Dee's mouth years ago
about Hilly, had actually happened to Dee, and backfired.

You must be careful what you do in life,
and be careful what you say;
because you reap whatever you sow,
just as sure as the flowers spring up in May.

PATIENCE AND FAITH TOGETHER

She was unable to bear children;
yet her heart longed for a child.
Her husband became angry
and left for a while.

She was sick with heartache
and cried 'til her eyes were reddened.
Asking God, "Why, oh why?"
for she was very saddened.

Her husband returned
after a month or two.
He begged for her forgiveness
as his head lay on her shoe.
She held him close
and said, "I forgive you,
but where have you been?"
for she hadn't a clue.

With tears in his eyes,
he admitted he had been faithful
while he was gone.
He stayed in a hotel
and stayed there alone.
He spoke with truth in his words.
She said, "Come, sit next to me,
and feel my stomach
because I am with a child, you see."

The night he left,
a child was conceived the day before.
They had already been blessed,
the day he walked out the door.

1 Thessalonians 1:2–3

We give thanks to God always for you all, making mention of you in our prayers, remembering without ceasing your work of faith, labor of love, and patience of hope in our Lord Jesus Christ in the sight of our God and Father.

—1 Thessalonians 1:2–3

VALUED TIME

Children are a valued blessing,
and their smiles warm your heart.
They bring joy and life in the home,
right from the start.

Their minds are like computers
storing everything they see and hear.
Teach them well, and
they will bring you much cheer.

Spend quality time with your children.
Read them books and stories.
If you fail to teach your children,
they will only bring you worries.

Teach and show them the wonders of nature, and
they will learn and grow to appreciate it.
Teach your son baseball, and
teach your daughter how to knit.
Spend time with your children
at home and at school.
Make time for family meetings,
and teach them rules.

Teach them the holy Bible,
and take them to church with you.
They will appreciate this in their adulthood,
and they will repeat the cycle with their children too.

Assuredly, I say to you, unless you are converted and become as little children, you will by no means enter the kingdom of heaven. Therefore whoever humbles himself as this little child is the greatest in the kingdom of heaven. Whoever receives one little child like this in My name receives Me. But whoever causes one of these little ones who believes in Me to sin, it would be better for him if a millstone were hung around his neck, and he were drowned in the depth of the sea.

—Matthew 18:3–6

A SLIP AWAY

How confusing life can be.
You think you're correct in your actions,
and you realize in a split second that
when you slipped, there was no traction.

Traction is a must in all aspects.
Without any grip, there is no control.
You must have traction
on the bottom of your soles.

There once was a couple
who never communicated with each other.
Their love evolved to hate,
and there was no more respect for one another.

Five years of marriage meant nothing to them anymore.
The man decided to walk away,
and he headed for the door.

He thought he had found love with another woman,
and he felt alive again.
He was a blundering fool
to succumb to the woman's grin.

He had left his wife.
The woman he had grown fond of
eventually left him,
and he was all out of love.

He couldn't go back home,
for he was ashamed and full of despair.
He moved out of the country,
feeling life treated him unfair.

The wife never heard from him again.
She went on with her life with many questions,
but she never looked back for him.
Life had taught her many lessons.

He who finds a wife finds a good *thing*,
And obtains favor from the LORD.
—Proverbs 18:22

GREED, ENVY, AND JEALOUSY

You thought she was an old fool.
You took that for granted.
But she never forgot the Golden Rule.
Now you walk aimlessly.

Your tail is between your legs,
Just like a dog whimpering and running.
Cracking all the golden eggs.

"Farewell," she said to him as a fake friend.
You were not a friend but of foe.
Even a deer knows where to find food.
Now you hang your head low.

Fall to your knees and call on Jesus.
He wants no one to perish.
Only you can make that call.
That's where you'll find your richness.

LOOK TO HIM

We find strength from God
to move the impossible.

We find peace from God
out of any chaotic situation.

We find comfort from God
when we are grieving.

We find discipline from God
who teaches us when to refrain.

We find wisdom from God
that no school could ever teach.

We find courage from God
who is our pillar of strength.

We find fullness from God
who fills us with the words of truth.

We receive blessings from God
who supplies us abundantly.

We find love from God
whose love is everlasting.

We find leadership from God
who guides and teaches us.

We find everything we need to know
in the holy Bible.

We find everlasting life from God
who promised us life in heaven.

God is almighty, above everything and everybody.
He even sent His only Son, Jesus, to die for our sins
so that we may have everlasting life with Him in
the holy kingdom.

A MADRIGAL
(A LOVE POEM FOR A
MUSICAL SETTING)

I spotted you in the crowd.
It had been a year since we first met,
and there you were.
My heart was racing like a jet.

We both came from different worlds.
Your world was neatly organized.
Your heart was that of a madrigal
that touched everyone's lives.

My world was so complex;
the timing always seemed to tick backward.
The time we spent together always
seemed to be awkward.

But the love that we had for each other
was always solid and true.
Love was the only thing
that we always held onto.

It was really good to see you again,
to see your award-winning smile,
which always captured my heart
attached to your unique style.

We always understood each other,
even when we were mute.
We answered with our eyes, while listening
to the symphony of flutes.

Could this be love, or were we just infatuated?
Did our hearts speak the truth of how we felt?
Finally, we played the hands
that we had been dealt.

As we walked down the matrimonial aisle,
I looked up at you, and I'll always remember
your award-winning smile.

OUR SOLDIERS AND VETERANS

Our veterans and our active soldiers,
Have lost their lives in battle.
My heart mourns for each one
There is no time or place for baffle.

Nothing is baffling to our brave soldiers at war.
They did what they had to do,
to stay alive to fight by their brothers
they worked as sisters and brothers, as one crew.

They have a tight knit formed
With each other.
They considered themselves
As sisters and brothers.

Let's not forget them.
Keep them in your prayers and thoughts.
They sacrificed much for us
As they stood side by side and fought.

Many have recently been sent home.
Thousands lost their lives.
The sacrifice they have made,
Widows for their husband or wives.
But we will remember them for the rest of our lives.

Continue to pray for our soldiers.
There will always be
A special place in our heart
For them, you see.

They are the backbone of our country
And the backbone to our families
And the United States citizens.
'Cause the soldiers keep us free.

They sacrificed their lives
To make sure we have peace.
My heart goes out to them
For they are our golden fleece.

BEWARE

He was a devil in disguise
That loved to torment people
With all of his inner lies.

He would befriend you
And hide his true self.
All the time plotting,
Piling dirt on your shelf.

He would copy and mold himself
Into people or actors on TV.
He was a sociopath!
And conniving as he could be.

He dressed as a sheep
But inside, he was a wolf.
Ruining lives frequently even when he was sleep.

The real devil that he is.
People began to see
For what he really was.
Only then you'd be set free.

Set free from the evil one.
That demised people for years.
Then people began to see
And they ran as quick as deer.

Beware of some people
Who dress in disguise.
These kinds of people are out to hurt you
'til you finally open your eyes.

A SPECIAL SOMEONE

Love is in the air
For a special man in my life.
This is the first time I found someone,
That I would love to be his wife.

He's handsome and intelligent.
His intuition is razor-sharp
And he carries himself as a man.
His wisdom are words of a harp.

He's slow to anger
And quick to forgive.
This makes him extra special,
For this is important to live.

The world needs more caring people
And less violence and hate.
Yet some people have to choose
Their own destiny and fate.

Do not entertain your mind
To what you know what is wrong.
Entertain your mind to what is right
And your life will be long.

POINTING YOUR FINGER

Don't make faces at anyone
Or point your finger.
Point them back toward yourself
Or it will come back to bite you and linger.

Don't frown or gossip
When someone runs on bad luck.
Cause it'll bounce back to you
And you'll find yourself stuck.

What goes around
Comes back to you for judging.
Stand up firm and don't be a clown.

Clowns are to make people laugh.
People are to encourage others.
What you do will be done to you,
So love your sisters and brothers.

Don't try to make people feel low
When you feel you are up high
Wishing for what you want.
Maybe that one person may say goodbye
And that may be the person
Who would help you.
But you are too blind to see that
So don't let that happen to you too.

SOFTNESS

Softness was in her eyes
When she spoke to me.
The aura around her was noted.
She was touched by an angel that also touched me.

We both felt the presence
That the Lord was in us.
The Holy Spirit was in our midst.
This was beneficial for our souls in us.

Heavenly things changed,
How we talked, thought, and walked.
There was nothing but joy and peace
Among us when we talked.

Sometimes if you feel the Holy Spirit,
Be still, quiet, and listen
And your spirit will absorb it.

LONELINESS

If you are single
And live alone,
Although you may get lonely,
You are not alone.

But loneliness is not a bad thing.
You have family and friends.
Do some volunteer work
And this is where loneliness ends.

Use your God-given talents
To utilize them for happiness.
This helps others as well,
With this, you don't have to second-guess.

Being alone can also be a good thing.
'Cause you may have a spouse or friend,
That brings hell in your household.
Keep your house peaceful; make this your trend.

Ask Jesus to send that special someone
Who will fill your house with happiness.
Take this rightful path with Him,
And that special someone will not treat you like a toy.

Keep the Lord in your midst
And never give up for what is right.
Use the gifts He gave us
And only then you will see the light.

The light will shine in your eyes,
Mind, spirit, body, and soul.
And others will see this
All in one bowl.

The bowl of life and happiness,
Which He entitles us to have.
Stay on the right track
And this will lead you to your destiny and path.

TEACH YOUR CHILDREN

Violence with young people and teens
Are way out of whack.
It all starts at home
Teach and discipline them so they won't fall through the crack.

Mothers and fathers, do your part as parents.
Even if your child resents it,
You'll be giving them values and rules.
This will also help them in schools.

Know where you children are at all times
Look for them and bring them home.
Before something happens to them
And you're left all alone.

Go to your child's school,
Do this week to week
'Cause the surprise visits
Will help the teachers teach.

I had to do these things.
My children resented that.
But I did what I had to do
And that's a fact.

Keep a tight rein on your children.
Sometimes you have to punish and reward kids.
For doing the right thing at home or away from home,
This will keep them from a deep skid.

My children are adults, and I'm very proud of them.
Now they have children of their own.
They are wonderful parents and this will stick with their children
Even after they are all grown.

LIFE WITH YOU

I can't imagine life without you
You are an important love in my life.
I am whole with you and would be,
Only half without you in my life.

My love for you is deeper than deep.
With you in my life,
I would take that leap.

The leap of happiness and joy.
I never thought I could feel this way,
'Til you walked into,
My life one day.

This simple poem,
Is how I feel about you,
And my heart feels that it's right too.
This poem is to say I love you.

CLOSING

There were times when I felt this book would not be published, and other times I was adamant to continue writing. Then I felt in my heart that Jesus wanted this book to be done. So Jesus was my driving force in my faith to continue.

I encountered many trials and tribulations through the years, and I know now the reason for it. Sometimes we have to encourage ourselves and keep the faith, and sometimes we have to encourage others too. Little did I know when I started writing this book that is was all for a reason. God always puts the right people in your midst at the right time. All His works are perfect, and He makes no mistakes. I thank God for everything because He stayed with me no matter what my mistakes or flaws were.

When I was in my teens, I wrote a poem and mailed it to a publishing company. The publishing company responded that they were not interested at this time but for me to stay in touch for future poems. That was decades ago, and I didn't write another poem until I was thirty-eight years old.

Last November, I met Mr. Jim Cox of KEZK radio station. Jim offered his assistance to help me with my first published book. I feel that if Jim had not taken an interest in my book, I would not be writing this one at this time. He offered me an abundance of encouragement and interviewed me on one of his morning talk shows.

I listened to Mr. Cox for years on the radio. His voice was of intelligence, honesty, and sincerity. I thought to myself that if I ever write a book, this is the man that I want to interview me. I did not know that God was listening.

God always listens and answers our prayers accordingly.

> A man's heart plans his way, but the LORD directs his steps.
> —Proverbs 16:9

Let your conduct *be* without covetousness; *be* content with such things as you have. For He Himself has said, "I will never leave you nor forsake you."

—Hebrews 13:5

Thank you for reading this book, *Hope from Violence*. I pray that this book will give you strength and encouragement and draw you closer to our Father, Jesus Christ, and the Holy Spirit. "Ask and you will receive." He will meet all our daily needs and spread an abundance of blessings for you, your family, and the people you meet in your everyday contact. GOD BLESS YOU!

The ultimate!
You're born after a couple of years
You toddle around
And shed many tears.
After a few years.

You go to school
And learn many things.
At home, you learn the golden rules.
Some years have past
Then you are in junior high.
The peer pressure intensifies.
You're either straight, or you learn to get high.
Now you're in high school.
You look at the opposite sex more.
Some teens even date each other
And you realize they're nice or rotten to the core
Aaaah! Prom night is here
As the years go by.
You are either in college or married.
Or just lying around as life passes you by.
Now you're about thirty.
Then you're about forty years old
And your children are in paragraph five
And some of your old friends
Are either dead or alive.
Have you lived life to its fullest?
Did you make a difference in the world?
Or sleep all those years?
As countries changed and so did the world.
Don't blame others for your mistakes in your life.
Others never walked in your shoes.
It's your choice to choose your life if it will be good or full of strife.

This book is dedicated to all the first responders.

THE PAST AND THE FUTURE

As I look back in the past,
I often wonder where did spring go.
How did summer and fall pass,
and winter is in full blow?

How cold the air is.
How cozy the cold can make the air crisp.
The smell of fresh snow
against my cold, chapped lips.

I look back and often wonder,
How did four seasons come and go so fast?
I often wonder what the future has.

Some things are meant for us to know;
some things are a great mystery.
But the things that become visible
we are meant to see.

LOVE VERSUS HATE

It took me three decades to know
I was not put on this earth
To please people
I was put here to help people since birth.

Now that I know this is my heart
It has changed my world in this life
Even though some people hated me
That meant they hated themselves and their life.

Life is what you make it to be
It is never too late for anyone
To change hate to love.
Only then you will learn you have won.

You've won the love of God
When your soul feels right by him
Don't allow hate to win you over.
'Cause it will send you away from him.

Please read John 15: 18–25. After you have read this, let it sink in, and you will have the opening of the eyes, heart, body, and soul, which will be very fulfilling to you as an individual and to others too.

I have to add in this book the best orthopedic surgeon in America. His name is Dr. C. I do not have permission to write his name, but because of him, I am no longer in a wheelchair every day. Dr. C has gifted hands and a gifted heart. Because of him, hundreds, if not thousands, have been helped and ushered for a better life. I met him and his wife at a book signing and haven't seen him in years. His outstanding demeanor is still steadfast along with his beautiful wife. God bless you, Dr. C, for everything you have done for me and all your patients. Your skills, doctrine, and heart are truly blessed along with your family. I hope to meet with you and your wife again. It was such a pleasure to see you both.

I thank you for purchasing this book, and I pray it helps you with a lot of guidance and assistance with life's troubles. The good, the bad, and the ugly will make us or break us. Instead of it breaking you, break through 'til you find the good because it is there.

Thank you for purchasing this book, and God bless you.

Darlene Jamison, Retired nurse administrator,
retired first responder volunteer nurse, artist, author,
and fundraiser for different organizations.

CLOSING

I've had several people tell me that the last book I wrote, *The Silent Patient*, and this book, *Hope from Violence*, will be made into a movie because these two particular books are so compelling that it may become one of the best movies of this century. I respond to them that if it is His will, it will be done.

If you need a great attorney and need diligence for truth of an injury outcome, Mr. Daniel J. Gauthier is the attorney to call at (314) 726-1817. God the Father, God the Son, and God the Holy Spirit brought some of the most helpful and loving people in this world in my life for me to meet and know. For this, I will always be thankful for all those who sincerely love me with their heart.

ABOUT THE AUTHOR

Darlene Jamison currently resides in St. Louis, Missouri. She is a retired nurse, a retired first responder volunteer, and a retiree from four local help agencies. Now she is an author and artist which she enjoys during her retirement years.

Her hobbies are listening to soft music, and she loves country music. Also, she enjoys helping others in need, fishing, and watching true story-movies, including Western and true war movies. All the books she has created and will create will always be true stories for people to learn that nothing is impossible and to help them along the way. But everything is possible through God the Father, God the Son, and God the Holy Spirit.

She was told that she would not live this long, but God is so awesome. He has much more work for her to do in His name. She is not here to please anyone but God. She advises everyone to please stay in school and go to college, but the best college to go to is the Holy Bible because God teaches better than man because He is holy. To be a student of God brings you to be a man of God. He will bless you with astronomical wisdom that can only come from him.